MW00931743

YOU WILL ROCK AS A DAD!

THE EXPERT GUIDE TO YOUR BABY'S FIRST YEAR AND EVERYTHING NEW FATHERS NEED TO KNOW

YOU WILL ROCK AS A DAD!
BOOK TWO

ALEX GRACE

© **Copyright 2024 - All rights reserved.**

The content contained within this book may not be reproduced, duplicated, or transmitted without direct written permission from the author or the publisher.

Under no circumstances will any blame or legal responsibility be held against the publisher, or author, for any damages, reparation, or monetary loss due to the information contained within this book, either directly or indirectly.

Legal Notice:

This book is copyright-protected. It is only for personal use. You cannot amend, distribute, sell, use, quote, or paraphrase any part, or the content within this book, without the consent of the author or publisher.

Disclaimer Notice:

Please note the information contained within this document is for educational and entertainment purposes only. All efforts have been executed to present accurate, up-to-date, reliable, and complete information. No warranties of any kind are declared or implied. Readers acknowledge that the author is not engaged in the rendering of legal, financial, medical, or professional advice. The content within this book has been derived from various sources. Please consult a licensed professional before attempting any techniques outlined in this book.

By reading this document, the reader agrees that under no circumstances is the author responsible for any losses, direct or indirect, that are incurred as a result of the use of the information contained within this document, including, but not limited to, errors, omissions, or inaccuracies.

CONTENTS

INTRODUCTION

Remember the day you stared down at those two pink lines on the pregnancy test, your heart racing with a mix of excitement and terror? Fast forward to what seemed like both the longest and shortest nine months of your life, and you're now in your baby's first year! How time flies! Every first-time dad has felt that rush of emotions, wondering if he's up to the task or feeling like he has absolutely no idea what he's doing. The truth is, you likely don't have a clue about what you need to do or how you should do it. And how could you? For the first time, you're suddenly responsible for a brand-new life and may even wonder how such big hands will be able to handle such a tiny body.

For many men, including myself, fatherhood starts out feeling like an emotional rollercoaster that you both enjoy and fear. In an attempt to become the perfect dad, you might rush online to research everything you need to know. Unfortunately, due to the vast amount of information and opinions just a click away, you're most likely left feeling more unsure of what to do than ever before. Many of your family members or friends may also offer their well-meaning but unsolicited advice, which might completely go against what you read online. This may leave you feeling like you're drowning in confusion, completely overwhelmed.

You may deeply fear the loss of your identity and time. The transition from having ample personal time to dedicate most of it to a newborn is drastic. Gone are the days when you could simply stop at the local bar for a beer with your friends, get in a good long session at the gym, or just spend some alone time whenever you want, without having to rush home to fulfill your share of the parenting duties.

This feeling of being trapped in your new role in which you likely doubt your own capabilities and adequacy can easily lead to "new dad anxiety." You may deeply fear making mistakes, not being supportive enough for your partner, or not bonding properly with your baby. You may even question whether you can do it at all as you must suddenly become an expert in changing diapers, handling throw-ups, or soothing a crying baby at 3 am.

While all these changes in your life are taking place, you may also fear the future of your relationship with your partner. Before becoming parents, you could simply enjoy spending time in each other's company without sharing the other with anyone. With the arrival of a new baby, the dynamics in your relationship with your partner can change drastically. You may worry that your sex life may be over forever, as both you and your partner may be too tired or overwhelmed to even think about getting it on, especially during the stressful early months of parenthood.

Luckily, these overwhelming fears over your new role and responsibilities don't have to take away from the joy fatherhood can bring. You can become the type of father you've always believed you could and will be. By becoming more intentional with the role you play, your involvement, and the impact you have on your child's life, you will empower not just yourself but also your child to thrive.

In the second series of *You Will Rock As a Dad!* we will be discussing everything you need to know from practical advice on baby care to the emotional and psychological challenges new dads face. This will help to ensure you feel supported, informed, and ready to embrace fatherhood, as it will answer all those burning questions about the first year and offer real solutions to those everyday baby challenges.

ABOUT ME

I am very excited to be helping you along your new journey. If you've read my first book, I want to say welcome back! If you are new to the "You Will Rock As a Dad! Series" I want to say "nice to meet you, new dad!" A little bit about me, I've grown up in a sports family where teamwork and collaboration ruled the house. I enjoyed the role of "fun uncle" for many years before I became a father. I thought I would easily ace the new role, as over the years, I was the go-to family member for my nieces and nephews, and had extensive background within the childcare system. I thought to myself, "if I love being around children, surely having my own would be a piece of cake."

Unfortunately, I didn't anticipate the absolute shock to the system that becoming a dad could bring. It's not like working in childcare where you could have fun teaching and guiding children but then send them home to their parents at the end of the day while you enjoy the freedom of blowing off steam. Suddenly, you need to become the responsible one who has to put your child and family above anything else.

After I eventually overcame this shock and learned to manage my high levels of "new dad anxiety," I decided to focus on doing the little things right. That helped to take the stress out of the tasks and before I knew it, I settled into my new role and already started nagging my wife to try for another baby, full of dreams of creating my own little sports team at home.

Now, I want to help you. I am passionate about sharing my knowledge and experience with other dads to make this journey not only easier but also more enjoyable for them. You may have already started this journey with me in my debut best-selling book, *You Will Rock As a Dad! The Expert Guide to First-Time Pregnancy and Everything New Fathers Need to Know*. In this book, we discussed everything you need to know about being the perfect partner to your pregnant counterpart (and score massive brownie points in the process). Now, we'll focus on the first year of your baby's life and how you can go from being an average Joe to a true super dad for your little one. So, grab your cape, and let's get started. Because one thing is for certain, now that we are on this journey together, I know you will rock as a dad. Better yet, when you're done reading this book, you're going to have what I like to call, "rockin' dad energy". The dad jokes are starting!

Let's dive in.

BONUS ACCESS

Oh, and 1 more thing before we begin! I made you this exclusive and absolutely free cheatsheet guide "Calm the Crying: 7 Simple Tips to Soothe Your Baby Quickly".

If you feel you've been struggling to calm your baby, this is for you!

Scan the QR link below to access immediately.

SCAN ME

Now the wait is over. Let's officially dive in!

CHAPTER ONE

EMBRACING THE CHAOS OF LIFE WITH A NEWBORN

R emember those calm Sunday mornings, coffee in hand, peacefully browsing through the news, or bingeing your favorite series? Your baby, with their round-the-clock demands, has different plans for you! Welcome to the first month of fatherhood, where 'unexpected' is the new norm. But here's a secret: It's the most fulfilling chaos you'll ever embrace.

If you are prepared for the challenges that you may face during this whirlwind of a month, you'll empower yourself to handle anything, regardless of how unexpected it may seem. This will help you to make sure your brand-new family thrives.

FROM EXPECTATIONS TO REALITY

Being a dad involves far more than simply sowing your seed and letting your partner squeeze the life out of your hand during childbirth. It also involves much more than just working to financially provide for your family. In today's world, the traditional notion of men being the sole breadwinners while women solely manage childcare and household tasks is a thing of the past.

These days, it's common for both parents to work full-time, which means all household chores and parenting duties ideally are split between both parents. You both won't just have to provide for your family financially but also play an active role in the daily running of your home and raising your child. The demands placed on dads in modern life are becoming more than ever before, which can easily result in feelings of guilt over either not bringing in enough money for their partners to stay at home, if their partner chooses to, or not contributing enough to the household on an emotional level.

Research done by Lancaster University found that men also don't get the credit they deserve for their role in caring for their children (Brindle, 1999). Families mostly focus on the bigger tasks, such as cooking, caring for young babies, and helping older children with homework. In many homes, these are tasks that are fulfilled by the mothers, while many dads are regarded as the "fun parent" who play games with their children, help them with sports, or drive them to and from activities. Even though they play an important role in their children's lives, the input of mothers is often regarded as more important.

Unfortunately, the business world has yet to catch on to the change in parenting roles of modern-day dads, compared to the previous generation. Many companies still discriminate against men who want to take parental leave when their children are sick or have an event to attend at school.

Social media can make things even worse, particularly when you start to compare your parenting style and influence as a dad to what you see on social media. People seldom post the truth about their lives. Instead, what makes it onto social media pages are often heavily edited videos or photos. You may admire the dad in the laughing videos while he plays sports with his son in the park or quick selfies of stroller rides. But, what you don't see are the tantrums that happen when the son accidentally steps in dog feces during the mini-football match or how the dad had to carry his son down the street as he suddenly got too tired to move but had the energy to kick and scream while being carried off. So, when you compare yourself and your role as a dad to what you see on social media, you'll often compare yourself to an idealist view of fatherhood, which is far removed from reality.

When you're involved in your children's upbringing and share the parenting duties, you'll not only have a happier partner but your children will also reap the benefits. Studies have found that children whose fathers are actively involved in their lives generally do better at school, are healthier, are more disciplined, and have a reduced risk of getting themselves in trouble with the law (FamilyEducation Editorial Staff, 2022).

THE POWER OF PATIENCE: ACCEPTING THE UNEXPECTED

I'm sure you've seen this scene play out a few times: A father is standing in line at a store with his toddler throwing a full-on tantrum, wanting a new toy or candy. At first, you can see the father is trying his best to stay calm and not give in to the tantrum. However, after a while, his patience runs out and he either loses it by scolding his child and dragging them out of the shop, or giving in to the tantrum and buying his child the toy or candy they wanted to begin with.

Before your child gets to this level of unrelenting and strong-willed public performances, you might have planned how you're going to deal with them and stay calm at all times. I was one of them. I always believed I knew how I would handle my children when they would throw tantrums. Unfortunately, I had no idea what I was in for and I soon realized that my plans were often just as ridiculous as the reasons for their behavior. Just like the gas in my car, I ran out of patience too many times, because I never prepared myself to accept the unexpected. And, just like it's necessary to have that gas in your car if you want to drive somewhere, patience is a necessity in parenthood. Unfortunately, this is something many parents lack.

So, before we go any further, let's first look at patience. The Merriam-Webster dictionary defines being patient as "going through your struggles calmly and without complaining about what's happening, or remaining steadfast despite the struggles you may endure" (*Patient*, n.d.). When you're a parent, especially when you're just starting on this journey, you may struggle to cope with some of your challenges, which can include difficulty consoling your crying baby, burning dinner because you're busy tending to your child, dividing your chores and duties with your partner, or even just the lack of freedom that typically comes with having a newborn in the house. When you respond to these challenges by showing your irritation, complaining, or yelling, you'll only end up increasing your stress levels, which will make the situation significantly more difficult (speaking from experience here).

While there are many ways in which you can work on becoming more patient, I found a combination of accepting there will always be unexpected events and seeing the bigger picture in everything you do. Once I was able to change my mindset from trying to fight the unexpected events to simply accepting that there would always be things out of my control and that I needed to go more with the flow, I was able to become more emotionally stable, even in these difficult times. In my view, patience is a combination of both your attitude in how you choose to see things and your ability to choose how you want to respond. Simply put, patience is broken down to attitude and response. Until the big corporations figure out how to bottle and sell patience (I know many parents who are desperately hoping for that to happen), becoming more patient will require continuous effort.

Think of your approach to fatherhood as a toolbox; your attitude is the key tool that can either build a solid foundation or create obstacles, similar to self-fulfilling prophecies. If you go into parenting believing you won't have the patience to deal with the many instances that will test your patience, then I can almost guarantee you that your patience will fail you more often than not. No matter how much we might want to have it all, parenting comes with many sacrifices that may seem hard to make now but will be well worth it in the end. So, if you start this journey with an open mindset and accept the unexpected, you will be able to deal with your challenges a lot more effectively.

When you choose to see the bigger picture, you'll realize that this challenging moment that's currently testing your patience is nothing but a small irritation in your bigger journey. You don't have to turn it into a massive road bump that will damage your relationship with your partner or your children. Instead, if you can embrace the power of patience, you'll build the foundation for lifelong happiness with your partner and children.

For the first week or so after bringing our first baby home, I was bursting with pride. I was incredibly proud of my wife for sacrificing her body to bring a new life into the world. I was proud of my role in creating this life. And, I was so in love with our baby that I would spend hours looking at him, counting his 10 toes and fingers repeatedly. I was also very impressed with how well he slept at night, (at first), thinking we were going to ace parenthood.

Alas, our home's brief stint of solitude had an expiration date shorter than a microwave popcorn timer. Soon, our sweet little baby discovered his lungs and voice, and my wife and I would spend many sleepless nights passing him to and fro between us, desperately hoping that the other one would have the magic touch to get him quiet. I'm not going to lie to you, this tested our patience and there were many times my wife and I wanted to both sit in a corner and join our baby in crying. In Chapter 4, we'll discuss tips on how to calm yourself and your baby during these difficult times.

While you need to stay patient with your children, you'll also need an extra bucket of patience with your partner. She has been to hell and back to bring a new life into this world, not just physically but emotionally and mentally as well. Now that there's a new life to care for, it's possible she may doubt herself and her ability to be a good mother. Don't we all a little when we're new at something? You need to be patient with her when she struggles to cope with her new duties and just doesn't get to the chores on her to-do list. Cut her some slack. Just like it's not easy being a first-time dad, becoming a first-time mother can be a terrifying but highly rewarding experience.

SKIN-TO-SKIN, BATHING, AND SUPPORTING THEIR NECK

During the first month of life, most of a newborn's movements are a result of reflexes, particularly in their arms, legs, and face. Yes, Dad, those sweet smiles that you may be so excited to see aren't actually smiles just yet, but keep looking and photographing. Their deliberate movements will mostly be around sucking and swallowing. They may also turn their heads slightly in search of milk and if you put something in their hands, they may grasp it. As your baby grows and their movements become more coordinated, keep a watchful eye on what they grab as there will come a time when they'll put everything they touch in their mouths, even a dirty old rag.

They won't be able to see anything further than a few inches from their faces, so hold your baby as often as you can, particularly when they're awake, to help them connect your face with your voice that they'll know so well by now. By the end of the first month, they should be able to focus on still and sometimes moving objects. If you've been placing your baby on their tummy regularly for tummy time, they may be able to lift their heads off the ground by the end of the first month. We'll also discuss tummy time in more detail in Chapter 4.

During the first few months, your baby will spend most of their time sleeping. In fact, most newborns sleep for up to 16 hours a day. Unfortunately, this won't be a straight sleep cycle. Most newborns won't sleep longer than 30 minutes to an hour at a time. They may also confuse their day and night sleep cycles. We'll discuss tips on how to improve your baby's sleep cycle later in this chapter.

You should never be afraid of picking your baby up. Yes, their bodies may seem small and fragile but they are a lot stronger and tougher than they may seem. The most important thing to keep in mind is to always support their necks when you pick them up. At this stage, the muscles in their neck will be too weak to support the weight of their head. You can do this by always keeping one hand under their necks when you pick them up, and supporting their bodies by placing your other hand under their butt.

Never shake your baby, whether during play or in frustration. This can result in shaken baby syndrome, which basically means bruising or damage to the brain bouncing back and forth in the skull. In severe cases, shaken baby syndrome can cause brain damage or even be fatal. When you place your baby in their stroller, car seat, or any other chairs you might have for them, you should always strap them in securely to keep them safe and prevent the likelihood of this syndrome.

Building a strong bond can begin right from the moment your baby arrives by gently cradling them, caressing their tiny bodies, or providing a soothing massage. Skin-to-skin contact can also hold many benefits, such as calming your baby, regulating their body temperature, and even boosting their immune system. To do this, take off your shirt and let your baby, dressed in only their diaper, lie tummy-down on your chest. If you want to flex some muscles to impress your partner with your new "dad bod," go for it (sarcasm intended here!).

During the first few days, your baby only needs sponge baths. This is to ensure their umbilical cord stump stays as dry as possible so that it can fall off. If your baby was circumcised, you'll also want to keep their penis as dry as you can until it heals. Once you can bath the baby, get everything ready before you take them to the bathroom (or baby bath, if you wish to wash them in the room.) Always add cold water to the bath first before you top it up with hot water until you get the desired temperature. This is to avoid burns in case your baby accidentally comes in contact with the water. Make sure you have their body wash, face cloth, cotton balls, towel, clothes, diaper, and diaper clean ready.

When you place your baby in the bath, support their neck with your hand and use your middle finger and thumb to keep their ears closed and reduce water entering their ear canal. Use new cotton balls to clean the skin around their eyes, a fresh one for each eye. After that, you can clean their bodies while always supporting their necks.

Remember, every baby is unique and may not follow these general guidelines or tips exactly. If you have any concerns about your baby's development or behavior, it's always a good idea to consult with a healthcare professional.

FEEDING 101: BREASTFEEDING VERSUS FORMULA

During the first six months, milk will be your baby's primary food source. After that, you'll gradually start to introduce soft foods while still giving them milk to supplement their feeds. This might sound simple enough but the milk you choose to feed your baby can be one of the first major decisions you'll make as a parent.

There are two options of milk for a newborn: breast milk and formula. While breastmilk will always be the perfect food for your baby, not all new mothers are able to breastfeed their babies. Some may have serious challenges, such as having inverted nipples or other medical conditions that may make breastfeeding impossible, while others may simply not get the hang of it or have enough milk for their babies.

My wife was really adamant about breastfeeding our children but she had many challenges. She first struggled to get the baby to latch and ended up with sore, cracked nipples. She went through many tubes of nipple cream to try to treat her nipples but she ended up bleeding through those cracks. Then, her milk never came in properly. As a result, our baby was underfed and his blood sugar dropped to dangerously low levels. The doctors gave her medication to try to increase her milk supply and recommended that she express milk—pumping milk out using either a hand pump, electrical pump, or even squeezing by hand—every hour while supplementing the feeds with formula. For the first three weeks of our first-born's life, my wife spent most of the time in the room expressing milk, only to gain two ounces of milk per day, which was barely enough for a single feed. To make matters worse, she developed a cold, which she passed on to our baby. His pediatrician then explained she had two options: Either continue in this way and risk our baby, who didn't have a strong immune system yet, getting sicker, or stop breast-feeding completely and treat her own illness. She was absolutely devastated and felt like she was failing our baby. Luckily, our baby thrived on formula.

After she gave birth to our second baby, she wanted to give breastfeeding a go a second time but struggled again with latching and not having enough milk. With the second baby, we made sure we had formula in the house as a backup in case we needed it. So, as we walked into the house after returning from the hospital, I walked straight to the kitchen to clean and sterilize the baby bottles. My wife made peace with the fact that she wouldn't ever breastfeed her children successfully. I was incredibly proud of how she handled this challenging situation.

Never force your partner into a specific way of feeding or make her feel bad if she struggles with breastfeeding. In a few years' time, your baby will put mud and dead insects in their mouths regardless of the type of milk you gave them as an infant. I remember one night as we sat down for dinner, our youngest child literally scooped up a dead fly with her mouth. I lost my appetite completely that meal. But, it just showed again that you should never put too much pressure on yourself or your partner on how you "should" feed your baby. As long as your baby is fed, you're doing a great job as a parent, not that I recommend feeding your baby dead flies, obviously.

Let's look at the pros and cons of each type of feeding, starting with breastfeeding. This will not only help your partner in making the decision on how to feed your baby but you'll also score serious brownie points with your knowledge of the different methods of feeding your baby.

All You Need to Know About Breastfeeding

Nursing a baby can be an incredible way for your partner to bond with your little one. Breastmilk contains all the nutrients and antibodies your baby will need, which can boost your baby's immune system and help their body fight off infections a lot easier. It's made up of different components, such as lactose, fat, and protein (whey and casein), which makes it easy for a baby's immature digestive system to digest the milk. This then results in fewer cases of diarrhea and constipation in breastfed babies.

Another benefit of breastfeeding is its practicality. Your baby's milk will always be ready for them at the perfect temperature, so no matter where you may go or how long you may be out of the house, as long as your partner is there, your baby can be fed. This can also make nighttime feeds a lot easier, as there will be no need to wash and sterilize bottles and bottle teats or warm up a bottle in the middle of the night.

Your financial situation can also impact your decision on how to feed your baby. Breastmilk is obviously free, whereas formula can do a serious number on your budget, especially if you didn't plan on buying formula to begin with. What's more, since breastfed babies' immune systems develop quicker, they will be less likely to get sick, which means fewer trips to the doctor, copayments for these specialists, or money spent on medication. Since babies have many needs that can easily cost hundreds of dollars a month, the cost of formula and other potential expenses are things that should definitely be considered when you decide how you want to feed your baby. Trust me, every cent saved can help a great deal when unexpected emergencies happen, such as if your baby needs fancy ointment for a skin condition or a nappy rash.

In general, breastfed babies adjust to eating solids a lot easier. This is because the taste of their milk will vary according to their mother's diet. Since they are exposed to different flavors a lot earlier in life, they tend to accept the different flavors of solids more easily as well.

Breastfeeding can have amazing benefits for your partner as well. If she's physically able to do this, it can give her confidence as a new mother an amazing boost. Breastfeeding can also help to shrink her uterus back to its pre-pregnancy size a lot quicker. Some studies suggest breastfeeding can lower the risk of high blood pressure, breast cancer, ovarian and uterine cancer, cardiovascular disease, and diabetes (Ben-Joseph, 2018).

Unfortunately, as was the case with my wife, many women struggle to nurse their babies or might not be able to do so at all. Some medical conditions, such as anything that requires chemotherapy, HIV/Aids, taking certain medications, or even some infections, can make breastfeeding unsafe for the baby. Also, women who have had any form of surgery on their breasts, which includes breast reductions and enlargements, may struggle more with breastfeeding.

Your partner's lifestyle should be considered when you make this decision. While it's a fact that breastfeeding can be very convenient as the milk is always ready for your baby to drink, breastfed babies typically drink a lot more often than formula-fed babies as they digest breastmilk a lot faster than formula: On average, newborns that are breastfed drink every two hours, while formula-fed babies can go for three to four hours between feeds. If your wife has to return to work shortly after having a baby and can't express milk or feed your baby every two hours, this type of feeding might not work for her.

New mothers who breastfeed should also take more care of what they eat or drink as everything they consume can be passed onto the baby. For example, fish can be a no-go due to the level of mercury it may contain, tomato and chocolate can make her milk more acidic, caffeine can cause restlessness in your baby, and alcohol—yes, even after giving it up for nine months, should still be off-limits for breastfed babies—can result in fetal alcohol syndrome, which can have serious and lifelong implications for your baby.

Formula: A Healthy Alternative

Formula is infant milk that's commercially prepared and contains most of the nutrients and vitamins contained in breast milk. Again, just like you need to set the right expectations for fatherhood, the formula that's available these days has evolved tremendously. If your partner can't breastfeed, your baby will do just fine with a good formula that contains all the proteins, fats, and sugars they need.

Formula feeding will require more preparations in that bottles need to be washed, sterilized, and warmed for your baby to enjoy. However, it does give a lot more flexibility. Feeding a baby when you're in public can be easier than breastfeeding as your partner won't have to search for a quiet space or worry about covering herself up as the baby drinks. Other people can also help with the feeds, which means you, as the father, can join in on the precious bonding time during a feed. If your wife has to return to work, sending formula with her to the daycare or to the day mother who will look after them is easier than having to worry about making sure you have enough expressed milk available for the day.

If you do go for formula, it's best to create a routine early on of washing and sterilizing bottles. You may want to get a few bottles so you don't have to wash immediately after a feed to have the bottle ready for the next one. Always making sure you have bottles ready can take some planning and organization but once you get into the rhythm of how you want to do it, you'll find it will become easier and easier.

Since formula takes longer to digest than breastmilk, they not only need to drink less often, as we've mentioned, but they also tend to sleep better and may even start to sleep through the night within the first few months. Your partner's diet won't impact your baby's nutrition if they are formula-fed.

Therefore, communication with your partner is key to planning what course of action is best for your child's feeds.

Unfortunately, no matter how much work is put into developing formula, none of the antibodies that are found in breast milk can be manufactured for formula. This type of milk, therefore, doesn't boost the baby's immune system like breast-milk does. It can also take time to find the right formula for your baby. There are many different formulas available and it can take a few tries before you find one that works for your baby. The wrong formula can cause constipation, gassiness, and even diarrhea. Your child's pediatrician or lactation consultant will be able to recommend a formula they believe will work best for your baby but even with their expert advice, it can be a lengthy and costly period of trial and error.

Always keep an open mind when it comes to feeding your baby. As was the case with us and my wife who really wanted to breastfeed, your initial decision may not be realistic. Accept the unexpected and if you need to change your feeding plans, do it without any feelings of guilt for you or your partner. Choosing between breast milk and formula is like deciding between a homemade chef's special straight from mom or a gourmet takeout option—both have their unique flavors but it's all about what suits you and your baby.

TEST YOUR NEW DAD IQ

Now that we've discussed everything you need to know to be a stand-out dad to your newborn, let's check what you can remember. If you struggle with any of these questions, refer back to the various sections in the chapter to refresh your memory.

1. How often should your newborn feed?
2. Why should you adjust your expectations?
3. Why is it important to accept the unexpected?
4. Is it okay to sit back and relax while your partner takes care of the baby and all the household chores?
5. Can you give your partner a glass of wine while she's breastfeeding the baby?

Now that you're diving deep into the unpredictable waters of the first month, you might be sensing some unfamiliar emotions creeping in. Some mix of excitement, fear, and over-whelming responsibility? All normal. Welcome to the world of "New Dad Anxiety." But don't fret my new friend; in our next chapter, we're diving deep into it, helping you navigate and emerge stronger.

CHAPTER TWO

THE MYSTERY OF "NEW DAD ANXIETY"

I'll never forget the day my wife and I announced our first pregnancy to our friends. While most of them immediately congratulated us, there was one friend who became white and even looked a bit nauseous. By that time, he was already a father of three, all under the age of four. I could actually feel him shaking when he shook my hand, and with a nervous smile, he told me, "Good luck. It's a rollercoaster."

At that stage, I thought he referred only to the exciting changes that having our first baby would bring to our lives. It was only after our baby was born that I understood the many dips this rollercoaster takes, which can easily result in mental health struggles, or as I like to call it, "New Dad Anxiety."

If you've already had a taste of this type of anxiety, please understand you're not alone. Did you know that up to 10% of new dads experience paternal postpartum depression, and many more encounter heightened anxiety? (Horsager-Boehrer, 2021). This isn't just about a few sleepless nights; it's a deeper concern that's often overlooked. There are many reasons why you may feel particularly anxious or even depressed during this time, such as extreme fears over your new role and whether you have what it takes to be a good dad. And, let me tell you, by the end of this book I know you will.

Unfortunately, if you don't find a way to navigate your mental health and manage your anxiety and depressive thoughts more effectively, you may rob yourself of the greatest gift anyone can ever get: Bonding with your new family. So, let's unravel the mystery behind "New Dad Anxiety" and understand you're not alone in this journey.

WHAT IS "NEW DAD ANXIETY?"

You may have heard about baby blues and postpartum depression, where new mothers are experiencing extremely low and sometimes even depressive moods. This typically starts within the first few weeks after giving birth and can last for up to 1 year. If your partner struggles with this, you should do your best to be extra supportive and attentive toward their needs. Or perhaps you might be the one who needs an extra hug at the end of a tough day. And, let me tell you, fellas, there's nothing wrong with admitting that.

Postpartum depression can also occur in dads, particularly by the time your child is three to six months old (Horsager-Boehrer, 2021). I prefer calling it "New Dad Anxiety," as that is how I experienced it. Working in child care and being a coach in multiple different sports (soon, my kids will pick up golf and pickle ball), I couldn't remember a time when I didn't look forward to one day becoming a dad. When my wife revealed those double-positive lines on the pregnancy test, I was happier than a cat in an endless yarn pit, and I've never seen a cat happier than me since my first teenage kiss! But, a few weeks after the birth of our son, I felt myself lying to my family and friends every time I responded with the standard "good" or "great" when they asked me how things were going.

The reality was that while my wife and I were getting by, things were challenging. I was struggling to manage my work, the endless supply of diapers to be changed and bottles to be washed, and then the more mundane stuff, like helping to cook meals and picking up the dog poop outside. There were days when I felt like just throwing away the dirty dishes instead of just washing them. I know I sound dramatic, but it's true. I was dog-tired (and you might be too, but it's okay). I felt like I was in over my head and going to work in the mornings started to feel like a day-long vacay.

I can't even tell you how many nights I lay awake (even though I desperately needed sleep in between feeds) worrying about how I was going to cope with everything I had on my plate, my relationship with my wife, balancing being a new father, trying to be a person, and raising an entire human being. The combination of my severe sleep deprivation and stress caused me to become extremely irritable. I got so bad that not even kicking a few soccer balls on an open field (this was always my way of relaxing) could help me become a likable person again.

One night our son was extra cranky. Perhaps he could sense my high levels of tension. My wife was exhausted, so I offered to take him. It wasn't like I was going to sleep any way. I tried everything to get our son to settle: I rocked him for hours, sang for him (in retrospect, my singing could've made him more upset), and gave him tummy rubs, but nothing worked. Around 4 in the morning, I lost it. I grabbed his bouncy seat, dragged it to the living room, and put a movie on the TV, loud enough to drown out his moans. Eventually, we both fell asleep.

When I woke up on the couch and saw my baby sleeping like a little angel in his bouncy chair, I felt like I'd officially earned the "worst dad in the world" trophy. I knew something had to change, but I had no idea of how to pull myself together. I pulled my phone out to research and was amazed to discover that many other new dads had similar experiences.

I remember reading some of the online posts I found out loud to my wife, telling her that I couldn't believe that paternal postpartum depression was actually a real thing. She didn't quite look as shocked as I expected her to be. Instead, she just told me that it's because there are too many men like me who shy away from properly acknowledging our feelings and fears. This is one of the reasons why I prefer to call it "New Dad Anxiety" rather than postpartum depression.

That day, I promised myself that I would change. I wanted to be better. I wanted to teach my son that it's okay to be scared or emotional at times. I wanted to be the role model he deserved. Gaining this understanding was life-changing for me, as it may also be for you. It might even have saved my marriage.

SIGNS OF "NEW DAD'S ANXIETY"

While there are many similarities between maternal post-partum depression and "New Dad Anxiety," such as fatigue and appetite changes, crying is one of the most common symptoms new moms experience. This is often not present in men, most likely because to a large degree, society has encouraged us not to cry, show emotion, or talk about our feelings. We are a strange species, aren't we?

As a result of this stone-age way many of us have been raised, our symptoms of "New Dad Anxiety" can often show up completely different, which can make it more damaging to those around us than if we could just muster the courage to openly talk about what we feel. Some of the most common symptoms of "New Dad Anxiety" include:

- Anger outbursts or violent behavior.
- Impulsive or risky behavior, which can include overconsumption of alcohol or usage of drugs.
- Severe irritability.
- Excessive worry.
- Panic attacks.
- Lack of motivation and poor concentration.
- Withdrawal from relationships.
- Not enjoying the things you used to like.
- Physical symptoms, such as digestion issues, headaches, stomach pain, and muscle cramps.
- Sexual dysfunction.
- Sense of impending doom.
- Suicidal thoughts.

If your partner experiences baby blues or maternal postpartum depression, you should keep an extra close eye on your mood. Studies found that the partners of new mothers struggling with these mood disorders are twice as likely to develop "New Dad Anxiety" than the new dads whose partners' mental health is good during this time (Villano, 2018).

CAUSE AND TRIGGERS: WHY DO WE FEEL THIS WAY?

Apart from being more likely to experience "New Dad Anxiety" if your partner's mental health is also struggling, there are many other factors that could contribute to your anxiety getting the better of you, such as:

Hormones: As your partner gets closer to giving birth, you will experience hormonal changes, particularly a drop in testosterone. This is your body preparing to nurture and care for your newborn. Unfortunately, the downside to lower testosterone levels can be feelings of depression, which can add to your "New Dad Anxiety."

Feeling disconnected: Your partner starts to bond with the baby while she is still pregnant and if she is on maternity leave after giving birth, she will spend a lot more time with your baby. This can result in you feeling excluded and disconnected from both your baby and your partner.

History of mental health conditions: If you have a history of anxiety disorder or depression, your risk of developing "New Dad Anxiety" will be greatly increased.

Sleep deprivation: It's no secret that parents of a newborn won't get the amount of sleep they may need to cope with the challenges that come with being a new parent. When we are tired, we tend to be more cranky, which won't help the state of our mental health at all.

Financial struggles: Babies can do a number on your budget, especially if there are unexpected expenses you didn't plan for. If your money is already tight before having your little one, these additional expenses can cause a lot of stress.

Changes in your relationship: There's no way to escape certain changes in your relationship with your partner. Together, you'll be responsible for a brand-new life, which naturally means less time together. Your baby's cries may also interrupt any alone time you might have planned to spend together, which can be very frustrating for both of you. While these changes can put even the strongest relationships to the test, they may also create an even deeper bond and love between you and your partner.

Lack of freedom: Your life will change drastically after your baby has been born. If you're used to doing your own thing whenever you want, it can be incredibly frustrating when you need to rush home after work to take care of your baby and do chores. Your time won't be your own anymore; it's best to accept this sooner rather than later.

Not getting enough support: If you aren't lucky enough to have a strong support system you can rely on during this time to give advice or look after the baby while you and your partner enjoy a much-needed break, your frustration levels may be even higher than normal. All the pressure will then be on you and your partner to not only take care of your baby but also support each other.

Not having time off: Many new dads are hesitant to ask for time off from work after the birth of a baby as they may fear that it may either make them seem weak or even it may affect their chances of getting a promotion. However, spending more time at home after the birth of your little one can do wonders to reduce your "New Dad Anxiety."

As if this list of potential causes isn't long enough already, you can add the many fears most new parents experience during the first few months of parenthood to it as well. Some of these emotional rollercoaster fears can include:

The unknown: Until you're actually a dad, you won't ever truly know what to expect or what it's like to care for a tiny little human. The reality is that until you've looked after a baby before, you'll likely have no idea how to do even the basics of diapering, burping, or even holding them properly. Whether you want to admit it or not, you're likely shaking in your boots. Just remind yourself that there have always been things in your life that you had to learn first in order to get good at it, such as riding a bicycle. I've been in that exact same position. I think it's safe to say that all first-time fathers have. You are, in fact, a "first-time" father. Now, having been through it a few times already, I know you will learn quickly how to do all your new tasks. Yes, the journey to the unknown can be scary but you will get through it the only way anyone can: one step at a time.

Failure: Nobody likes to fail, particularly when you so desperately want to be a good father to your new little one.

There will be many times when you'll doubt yourself or even make yourself believe you don't have what it takes to be a good dad. Always remember that as much as you'd like to be one, there is no such thing as a perfect dad. All we as fathers can do is try our best every day, learn from the mistakes that we make, and love our families.

Not providing for the family: I haven't met a single father who didn't want the best for his children. Unfortunately, many people measure this by how many things they can buy for them. I remember when I was dealing with the fear of not being able to provide enough, a good friend told me to just make sure they had food to eat, clothes to wear, and a warm bed to sleep in. As long as they have that, they'll be fine. He also joked that children spell "love" differently to adults. They spell it "T-I-M-E." I reminded myself of that every time I felt bad about not being able to buy them the latest hoverboard or gaming console. When I couldn't afford to splurge, I made up for it by spending quality time with them. That is, after all, another way of providing for your family.

Not bonding with your baby: As I've discussed, your wife started bonding with your baby long before the little one was born. It's only natural that this process will take slightly longer for you. But, never give up, no matter how long it may take to create this bond with them. Spend as much time as you can with your little one and be patient. That magical connection you're seeking will come, and it will be worth the wait, trust me.

STRATEGIES TO OVERCOME ANXIETY

While your "New Dad Anxiety" may be completely normal and even justified, there are many ways to overcome it. There was a time when I wondered if I would ever get myself out of the rut I was in. I was completely overwhelmed by the new life that I had wanted and helped to create. But, it doesn't always have to be this way. Doing research helped me to understand why I was feeling the way I did. What I discovered not only assisted me in finding strategies to overcome my worries but also helped me find joy in fatherhood:

I started opening up: I have always been one of those men who didn't like to talk about my own feelings. After struggling with my mental health as a first-time dad, I realized that this was one of the first areas I would need to work on. I was lucky to have many close friends who were also fathers at different stages of the parenting journey. I realized that I had a network of fellow dads who understood my struggles without judgment and could share tips that had helped them. Even though it was a bit scary in the beginning to become vulnerable in front of them—I couldn't pretend that I had no feelings anymore—I not only gained deeper friendships but I was able to work through my struggles. Well, most of them, any way.

I worked on my sense of humor: No, I don't mean racking up a full supply of dad jokes. Or, maybe I did do a little bit of that too. Instead, developing a solid sense of humor helped me to appreciate funny moments in life. It helped me to laugh when my son smacked me in the face with a baseball bat. Or, when I only realized once I was at work that I forgot to take the nail polish off that my daughter insisted on putting on for me. What's more, it helped me not to be so hard on myself and to live by the mantra that I am doing the absolute best I can.

I practiced self-care: When one of my friends asked me what I was doing just for myself, I couldn't answer him. Especially during the latter part of my wife's pregnancy, my focus was on her and making sure she was okay. Then, after the birth of our firstborn, I tried to help out as much as I could. I was rushing from work every day so I could spend as much time with them to bond and help out. When my friend asked about my self-care, I told him point-blank I wasn't going to be so selfish with my time. He quickly helped me realize that practicing self-care was not a selfish act, but absolutely essential to stay afloat. It's actually selfless, as when you are functioning properly, everyone around you reap the benefits. It's as the old saying goes, "You can't pour from an empty cup." I discussed this with my wife and we agreed on times we would both get a few minutes to ourselves. I believe this helped both of our mental health a great deal.

I became more mindful: When a fellow father first suggested that I should adopt mindful habits, I literally laughed out loud. I didn't have a good perception of mindfulness, simply because I didn't actually understand it. I always thought of mindfulness as a wishy-washy term people used to make excuses for themselves. He explained to me that it's simply a way of consciously directing your focus to the present moment to help you focus on what's truly important. Despite his lengthy explanations, my friend saw I wasn't taking him seriously, so he suggested we do a bet: If I was able to incorporate a specific amount of mindful techniques over a set period of time, I would win the bet and some prize money.

And, if I wasn't able to do this, he would win. My competitive streak came out, and I went all in. I won the bet but wouldn't accept the agreed-upon prize money; I couldn't put a price tag on the value I got from becoming more mindful. These are the habits that I'm still practicing today:

- **Meditation**:

No, my new friends, you don't have to sit on the floor with your legs crossed chanting "ohm" to meditate. You can meditate anywhere and at any time. I tried to go to the quietest place possible (which was mostly before my children woke up). Then, I would settle into a rhythm of deep breathing, and just sit quietly for a few minutes. If any thoughts popped into my head, I would take note and accept them without judgment before returning my focus to my breathing. There are many short five to ten-minute videos available online that will help you learn how to meditate. I do recommend that you start with short meditation sessions, such as five minutes. This way you won't set too high expectations as meditation, like any new skill, is a muscle that needs to be built.

- **Journaling**:

I always thought of journaling as something teenagers or middle schoolers given a prompt by their teacher do, until I gave it a go. I didn't use a traditional book-type journal but downloaded the Daylio app on my phone that would remind me to jot down my feelings, thoughts, and plans. The algorithms on the app would then determine what specific negative patterns I followed, particularly when it came to my moods, which helped me identify many of my triggers and challenges.

- **Exercise**:

I've always enjoyed a good workout but with a newborn in the house, it was challenging to find enough time to be active. Or perhaps, lack of time was just my excuse for when I didn't have the energy to go to the gym after not sleeping properly. I had to make the mindset shift to get active again and remind myself that working out doesn't always mean I had to go to the gym. I started doing exercises in and around the house and even incorporated my baby in these activities, such as doing sit-ups while he was lying on my chest or putting him in the stroller for a jog or walk around the park. Babies can be surprisingly great workout toys; my biceps have never been as big as when I used them as weights.

- **Eating well**:

Life with a newborn didn't do our nutrition any favors; it was just so much easier to order takeout than to cook healthy meals. Unfortunately, all that oil and salt depleted our energy even more. After searching on social media, we found someone in our area who sold healthier frozen meals for those nights we didn't have the time or energy to cook. We also decided to only keep healthy snacks in the house. Although hard at first, these small changes made a massive difference.

- **Cold showers**:

I've heard many gym fanatics swear by cold showers but I honestly never had the guts to try it, unless it was really hot out. When I researched this, I was amazed at the many benefits it can bring, not just for your physical health but also your mental toughness and boosting your mind-over-matter capabilities. Now, I try to start every shower with warm water and gradually decrease the temperature to as cold as I can handle. You'd be surprised at the energy boost you feel after.

- **Sleep better**:

While proper sleep might seem like an unattainable dream when you have a newborn in the house, you can make changes to increase your odds of getting the best possible sleep when you get the chance. We worked on making sure we set the right atmosphere in our bedroom, which included adding a blackout blind in front of the window, installing a new air conditioner, and downloading sleep sounds. We also created a rule not to use any screens for up to an hour before we planned on sleeping, as the blue light emitted from these devices can slow down your body's natural release of melatonin, the hormone that helps you fall asleep.

- **Partner check-in**:

When you're the parents of a newborn, your lives revolve around your baby and making sure all their needs are met. Unfortunately, this can create distance in your relationship with your partner. One of the ways my wife and I worked at overcoming this was to do weekly check-ins. We decided to do this on a Sunday afternoon while the baby was sleeping.

During this time, we would briefly talk about our week with a specific focus on what we appreciated about each what we'd like to continue doing. This not only helped us to discuss our relationship but also to focus on the positives with each other. In Chapter 6, we'll discuss more ways of keeping the spark in your intimate relationship alive.

As you've seen, none of these positive habits require a lot of time. Later in this book, we'll go into more detail on how you can steal a few minutes to take care of yourself.

BUILDING CONFIDENCE THROUGH SMALL WINS

When we think of our children and our role in raising them, we tend to think of the big moments. You may think of your baby taking their first steps or wondering whether their first word will be "mama" or "dada." You may already dream about going to your child's first dance recital, basketball game, or teaching them how to ride a bike. Perhaps, you've already started a college fund or savings account for their wedding. While all of these are important milestones in any parent's life, they aren't the only thing that contributes to your overall experience of parenthood. Instead, it's those little things that make it all worthwhile. And, it's also those small wins that boost your confidence and remind you that you're doing a great job.

I distinctly remember the day when the importance of focusing on the positives really kicked in for me. I had to go away for a few days due to work obligations. I never used to mind doing work trips before I became a father, even though I preferred staying at home with my wife. Once I cut that umbilical cord, things were different. As much as there were times when I felt I could do with a break, I never wanted to be away from home for too long. Not only did I not want to let my wife fly solo with the parenting duties but I also feared missing out on important milestones. As a result, I tried my very best to avoid and postpone work trips. Eventually, I ran out of excuses not to go away.

During this five-day trip, many of those traditional big parenting moments happened. My baby said his first word (which, surprisingly, was "dada"), he cut his first tooth, and he took his first step. I missed all of them. I felt like an absolute failure as a father. These were moments I was looking forward to for months and they all happened over a few days while I was out of town. Funny how that timing worked out, huh? My wife did send me videos but it just wasn't the same as actually being there. Naturally, by the time I came home, my son was on his second word ("mama") and I had to wait for more than a week of me continuously saying "dada" before he said it again.

It was at that same time when I so desperately wanted him to call me that I realized hearing him say that magical word wasn't the most important thing. I was sitting on the living room floor one night while he was playing with his noisiest toys. Those are the same toys that I would usually make "Go Houdini" because listening to the same ridiculous tune on repeat isn't exactly my idea of fun. However, after being away for a week, I could bear it again.

I took my eyes off my son for a split second to read an email that had just come through on my phone. The next minute, I felt his tiny hands pushing on my leg. When I looked down, he was busy climbing onto my lap. Once he made his way up, I had two of those small winning moments. First, it was listening to his laugh as he was repeatedly hitting me in the face with a teddy. Then, the biggest small moment of all: He pushed his head into my chest and just sat like that for a few minutes. It was his way of hugging me and at that moment, I couldn't imagine myself being prouder of him and my little family. I realized that missing those traditional important moments was okay since what does matter is the absolute love that lives in my home, despite the chaos we often have to live through.

That night, I decided that I would live more in the moment so that I could really appreciate those small wins in life. This mindset change also helped a lot in calming any "New Dad Anxiety" I still experienced, as I allowed the little moments to motivate me and remind me that even though it didn't always feel like it, I was being the best dad I could possibly be for my child. Celebrating our small wins together strengthened our bond as a family. We grew closer than ever before.

OVERCOME THE FEARS OF FATHERHOOD

While the tips we discussed above may already be enough to reduce your "New Dad Anxiety," you might need to do more, especially if you have very specific fears or triggers to work through. Let's discuss things you can do to overcome some of the most common worries you may face:

- If you worry that you won't be able to provide for your family, you may benefit from consulting with a financial planner to not only help you plan and save for the future but also budget effectively. There are also many free resources online as well as books on how you can earn extra cash, should you wish to go that route.
- If you don't have any friends who are dads, you can consider joining support groups for dads, either in your area or on social media. Also, keep in mind that once your child goes to daycare or school, you're bound to meet other dads who can become good friends in the future.
- If you fear parenthood is negatively affecting your relationship with your partner, it's best to talk to her openly and make plans together on how you can work through these challenges.
- If you fear that you won't be a good father, take some time to think about the type of dad you want to be or what good role models you have in your life that you might want to emulate. Think about what these fathers do or if you can, ask your role model for advice. Then, consider what you can do to bring you closer to the type of father you want to be.
- If you fear you won't have a strong bond with your baby, spend as much time with them as possible. Take charge of as many of the parenting duties as you can. We'll discuss bonding in more detail in Chapter 3.

If you or a loved one experience prenatal or postpartum anxiety or depression symptoms that intensify or last longer than a few weeks, talk with your doctor about possible treatment options. Always remember there is no shame in admitting that you need help. Instead, it should be seen as a sign of strength and love for your family.

TEST YOUR NEW DAD IQ: CHAPTER 2

Now that we've discussed "New Dad Anxiety," its many potential causes, and how you can overcome it, let's do a quick check to test your new dad IQ. If you struggle with any of these questions, refer back to the various sections in the chapter to refresh your memory.

1. Is it true that "New Dad Anxiety" affects many first-time dads?
2. Can you name some of the common causes of "New Dad Anxiety?"
3. Why should self-care be considered a selfless act instead of being selfish?
4. How can focusing on the small wins help you on your parenting journey?
5. If you fear not being able to provide for your family financially, should you go to the casino and take your chances at winning big?

You're steadily navigating the waters of "New Dad Anxiety," but what about the bond between you and your baby? Let's dive into the magical world of father-child bonding in the next chapter: Dad's Role: Bonding With Your Newborn.

CHAPTER THREE

DAD'S ROLE: BONDING WITH YOUR NEWBORN

Before the birth of our first baby, my wife and I spoke at length about how we wanted to raise our child. Regardless of how he would be born, the plan was always that my wife would do skin-to-skin contact as soon as possible and perhaps try to breastfeed the baby. Then, it would be my turn to hold him.

When it was time for the delivery, everything went close to perfect, until it was my time to hold him. Suddenly, I was a ball of nerves and the clumsiest I've been in my entire life. I've held many babies in my life but at that moment, I was so uncoordinated that I wouldn't be able to catch a giant beach ball (and as a coach in multiple sports who prides myself on my hand-eye coordination, that's saying a lot). I remember the look on my wife's face when she tried to hand our son to me. It was a complete mixture of shock and confusion, perhaps with a touch of disgust mixed in there.

After my wife tried a few times to unsuccessfully hand the baby to me, the delivery nurse intervened. She told me exactly how I should hold my body and placed my son in my arms. I'm not going to pretend that I didn't feel uncoordinated the next few times I tried to pick our son up but eventually, it became second nature. Soon, I was doing my part to bond with our baby.

You see, my new fellow friends, bonding isn't just a maternal thing; it's equally essential for dads. When you create this connection with your new little one, you lay the foundation for your future relationship and allow your baby to feel safe and secure in their daddy's arms. What's more, you're also boosting their brain development, as repeated human contact allows your baby's brain to release the different hormones needed for memory, thought creation, and even language (*Bonding and Attachment: Newborns*, 2018).

Speaking of language, did you know that a newborn can recognize their father's voice from birth and, by three weeks, a baby can visually distinguish their dad's face? So, go right ahead, fellas. Hold your baby, talk to them, stroke their soft skin, and be the loving, awesome, and rockstar dad I know you were destined to become.

DIFFERENT OPTIONS FOR BONDING

Bonding with your little one should start as soon as possible after birth, and within the first hour, both parents should have had the chance to hold the newest member of the family. Many medical professionals refer to these first 60 minutes as the "golden hour," as both you and your baby will be primed to form this bond.

This is also why most healthcare professionals involved in the birth will delay tasks like weighing and measuring your baby until after you and your partner have had time to hold the baby post-birth. Unfortunately, there may be many reasons why you might not be able to hold your baby immediately after they are born. This is particularly the case when there are complications. Should these complications be so severe that your baby has to go to the neonatal intensive care unit (NICU), it may be weeks before you can put your baby on your bare chest.

Speak to the nurses in the NICU about other ways you can connect with your baby. You might be able to hold their hands and feet or touch their head while they are in the incubator. Alternatively, you can talk to them while seated in their vicinity. This way your baby will still sense your presence even if you can't physically hold them.

While skin-to-skin contact has many benefits, as discussed in Chapter 1, let's now look at other ways in which you can bond with your little one. Since you're a first-time dad who might not feel qualified to bond with your baby, here are some suggestions to get you started:

- Respond as quickly as you can when your baby is crying. Many people believe you should teach a young baby to self-soothe or even that you'll spoil the baby if you respond every time they cry. I completely disagree with that; you can't spoil a newborn baby.

Also remember, crying is the only way your baby can communicate with you. It's their own, special language. So, when they cry, help them to feel secure by tending to their needs or identifying something that might be wrong.

- Touch, stroke, or cuddle your baby when you can. This will help them to hear your heartbeat, which will make them feel safe. On this note, remember that for the nine months of pregnancy, your baby heard your partner's heartbeat the whole time. Recreating this will feel familiar to them.

- Make lots of eye contact with your baby when you interact with them. Remember to hold your baby close to your face so that they can see you and connect your voice, that they'll know so well already, with your face.

- Apart from talking to your baby, you can also sing to your baby. They won't care that you're not a Grammy award-winning singer or if you mess up the lyrics to the song. Just hearing your voice will be enough for them. Also, the more your baby hears you sing or talk, the quicker their language ability will develop.

Even if you are a super dad in the attentive department and swoop in whenever they need you, it can take some time to properly bond with your little one. For some people, it can take a few weeks or even months before you and your baby will truly understand and know each other. If this is the case, don't put too much pressure on yourself or your baby. Your partner had a nine-month head start, so don't beat yourself up. Apart from spending as much time as possible with them to get to know their different reactions, you can't force the bond. Be patient and enjoy the time you have with your tiny human.

I will never forget the moment when I knew my baby recognized me. It was within the first month. I always tried to talk to and around him as much as I could so that he could learn my voice. I actually started doing this while my wife was still pregnant; I read that babies can hear voices from inside the uterus, so I was willing to give it a go. Every night as I scrolled through news sites on my phone, I would read the articles out loud.

The first week or so after my baby's birth, my wife and I were responding to every sound he made. Until the one day when it was clear he knew me. Yes, sure, he probably didn't know I was his dad, but he knew I was someone important to him and that he should feel safe in my arms. Nothing crazy about that day, as I was just holding him in my arms like I usually do. He had just woken up from a nap and was a little cranky. Shocker! While he was lying in my arms, he looked up at me. He studied my face so intensely like babies all know how to do so well, it felt like he was looking into my soul.

The more he looked at me and heard my voice, the more his whole body started to relax. Something changed in his eyes. He gave me the kind of look that screamed, "Wait a second... I know you!" It was like my face triggered his brain's lost and found department. He stopped crying. I'm not sure how long we sat like that with him looking up at me; a newborn baby's attention span is extremely short, so it probably wasn't long. But, in that magical moment, time stood still.

After that day, the moments when our son recognized us became more frequent. He was about a month old when he would smile at the sight of his parents. Soon after that, he would do proper belly laughs whenever I made funny faces. Fellas, these are heart-melting moments to look forward to and capture, which we'll discuss more in Chapter 7.

VARIOUS WAYS TO HOLD YOUR BABY

In the first chapter, we briefly touched on how to pick your baby up and the importance of always supporting your newborn's neck. My main issue came in how to actually hold my son. I suddenly felt like an octopus with way too many arms flopping around. Once I got the hang of it and gained more confidence in my new father role, picking up and holding my baby quickly became second nature. Soon, you will feel the same.

If you feel as clumsy and uncoordinated as I did when I first had to hold my baby, let's look at the different steps to turn you into a pro:

Step 1: Clean your hands. You should always make sure your hands are clean before you handle your baby. As I've mentioned, a newborn's immune system is still developing, so it's best to wash your hands thoroughly and, if possible, use a hand sanitizer. Also, request all your guests to clean their hands before holding your baby.

Step 2: Make sure you're comfortable. Before you pick your baby up, make sure you have everything you might need ready, especially if you're going to hold your baby for a long time, such as letting them nap in your arms. You might need a pillow to support your arm holding the baby (even though they are tiny, they can feel surprisingly heavy after a while) as well as snacks or water to sip on. Also, if you're planning on cuddling your baby for a while, go to the bathroom beforehand. I've tried to do a toilet trip while holding my sleeping baby in my arms and trust me, it's not as easy as it may seem.

Step 3: Support their bodies. As I've mentioned, you should always support your newborn baby's neck when you pick them up. Also, pay special attention to where the fontanelles (soft spots at the top of your baby's skull) are so that you don't accidentally bump against them.

Step 4: Decide on a position. After you've picked your baby up, you need to decide how you want to hold them. As long as you are supporting their necks and are under their butts, you can hold them in almost any position that feels comfortable and relaxing for you both. Here are some common positions you can try:

- **Cradle hold**:

This is one of the easiest ways to hold a baby, particularly when they are still very little, as it will free up your other hand to do things. Simply bend your arm and let your baby lie on it, supported by your chest. Your baby's head will be cradled into the crook of your elbow while your hand will support their bottom.

- **Shoulder hold**:

This position is great for doing skin-to-skin contact as well as burping your baby. Hold your baby in an upright position. Let their head and body rest on your shoulder and chest, almost as if they're looking behind you. If you're sitting back or lying down like this, both your arms can be free. If you're sitting upright, you can use one hand to support their necks, while the other one is supporting their bottom.

- **Belly hold**:

This hold can be handy when your baby is gassy, has stomach cramps, or even for burping them. Hold your arm out and lay your baby on your forearm with their head toward your elbow. Their legs will hang on either side of your arm. If you want to burp your baby or help them get relief from gassiness, you can gently rub their back either upward or downward.

Ultimately, as long as you don't drop your baby or hold them up by one foot and let their body dangle to the floor, you should be all right.

SHARING RESPONSIBILITIES: PARTNERING WITH YOUR SIGNIFICANT OTHER

In the same way, you need to adjust to caring for your brand-new baby, you and your partner will have to slot into your new roles, not just as parents but also as co-parents. The day you gain the responsibility of becoming a dad, that same day life as you know it will change. While this change can most definitely be for the better, it can take some time to get used to your new life and what is expected of you.

There were many days when I felt completely frustrated with my new reality. I couldn't make my typical stops after work or even do the things I used to enjoy. With a newborn whose immune system is still developing, you naturally want to spend more time at home to keep them safe from germs and bacteria. There were times when I felt like a prisoner in my own home; being closed up like that didn't work well with my extroverted personality. But, the days of struggle were outlasted by the absolute beauty of parenthood. I was amazed by my new family, and the love I experienced every day changed my life, for the absolute better.

Yes, I didn't have the freedom to come and go as I pleased anymore, and yes, I had a lot more worries, anxiety, and responsibilities, but that comes with growing up, as my father once told me. Looking at my baby and seeing what an amazing mother my beautiful wife was, made me forever grateful for the incredible blessings I had. Reminding myself of how lucky I was, made me appreciate my wife more than ever before. This made it easier to find ways of sharing the parenting load.

I wanted to help, not only to make it easier for my partner (because, let's face it, during the pregnancy and childbirth she more than did her part in creating our family), but also to bond with my baby. I only had a few days off at home after my son's birth and wanted to make sure I used this time as much as possible to bond with him. At that time, my wife was still trying to breastfeed so apart from helping with burping, I couldn't do much bonding then. After discussing how we could split our parenting responsibilities more, we decided that bath time would be daddy-son time. I loved having these few minutes alone with our baby which was a dedicated special time. Plus, it gave my wife a few minutes to just be a person and do something else.

Although breastfeeding does result in natural bonding time for your partner and your baby, you can find other times to bond with your little one, like I did with bath time. For example, you can bond while holding your baby or carry them in a sling while you move around the house. After your partner has finished nursing your tiny human, you can join in the fun by burping your baby. Many young babies swallow a lot of air while they're drinking, especially when they don't latch properly. Their digestive systems aren't strong enough to bring the gas up again, so they need help, otherwise these gases can cause them pain or discomfort. To burp your baby, you can either let them sit on your leg while supporting their neck, put them tummy-down on your lap, or let them lie tummy-down on your chest. Then, simply rub their backs in an upward direction to bring the gas up. Many people might suggest that you pat their backs as well. Yes, this does work but the patting motion can break the winds up, which can result in them having more gas to try and help them get rid of it.

However you decide to get involved in your baby's care, create your own rhythm that works for you and your partner. The way in which the two of you co-parent can have a huge impact on your baby. This will be their first taste of teamwork. Creating a peaceful environment where you and your partner support each other, will provide amazing teaching opportunities for your little one. The way you interact with your partner will be an example to your child on how to treat other people with respect and communicate courteously.

Every person's circumstances are different. You and the mother of your baby might not be in a relationship with each other, which can make co-parenting more challenging. But, this doesn't mean you can't still be involved in your child's life and raise them together as a team. If you are both committed to giving your child the love and affection from both parents that they deserve, you can make it work. Depending on the nature of your separated relationship with your former partner, you can discuss visitation arrangements. In cases of severe conflict, it might benefit both of you (and especially your baby) to seek the help of a social worker trained in family matters.

TEST YOUR NEW DAD IQ: CHAPTER 3

Bonding with your baby will help you build a strong connection with them and understand their cues a lot better. This will make it easier for you to tend to their needs. Let's do a quick check to test your new dad IQ. If you struggle with any of these questions, refer back to the various sections in the chapter to refresh your memory.

1. How long should you wait after your baby has been born before you start bonding with them?
2. Why is it important to make eye contact with your baby?
3. How can you bond with your baby if your partner is breastfeeding?
4. Why should you share parenting responsibilities with your partner?
5. Will your baby hate you for singing off-key to them?

As we unearth the beauty of bonding, we also recognize that the daily grind awaits! As a new dad, you're bound to be hands-on with parenting duties and tasks around the house. Up next, we're diving into how you can tackle day-to-day tasks with finesse and perhaps a touch of fun! Ready to master the daily dad duties?

CHAPTER FOUR
TACKLING DAY-TO-DAY TASKS LIKE A PRO DAD

DAD HALFTIME!

Hey dads-in-progress! Quick pause here. How you doing?

We're nearly halfway through **"You Will Rock As a Dad!: The Expert Guide to Your Baby's First Year and Everything New Fathers Need to Know"**.

Can you believe that?

You are growing your "fatherhood knowledge muscle" every second you read this book!

And just like a good halftime show, it's time to celebrate your progress and gear up for the next chapter.

Remember all those insights, humor, and practical advice you've experienced so far while reading this book?

We bet it sparked some "aha" moments and got you excited (or maybe a little bit of nerves) about fatherhood.

Here's the thing: **your experiences are valuable!**

Scan the QR code below to share your review.

By sharing your mid-book reflections with other expectant dads, you can create a wave of support and camaraderie.

Here's how:

• **Leave a review:** Share what stood out to you in the book so far. What resonated most? Did you have any "aha" moments?

• **Tell your story:** How is the book shaping your perspective on fatherhood so far?

• **Offer encouragement:** Your insights can inspire and equip other dads-to-be for the challenges and joys ahead.

Why share? Simple. Your words can…

• **Guide and reassure** other dads on this incredible journey.

• **Foster a sense of community** – knowing you're not alone can make all the difference.

• **Help future dads rock fatherhood** – by sharing your experience, you're paving the way for a confident and supportive generation of dads.

So, leave a review, share your story, and let's build a community of dads who are ready to rock fatherhood together!

Now I'll let you continue with Chapter 4.

TACKLING DAY-TO-DAY TASKS LIKE A PRO DAD

Caring for a newborn baby will require you to suddenly become an expert at doing things you've never had to do before. You may also have to make peace with the fact that there may constantly be a bit of an odor hanging in the air. My second baby had severe reflux and no matter how much we burped her after every feed or how many burp cloths we used to catch any spit up, we would always end up smelling like sour milk. Even changing into clean clothes didn't help as the odor seemed absorbed by our skin, and there just wasn't time to have a shower after every feed. So, fellas, I had to make peace with sour milk being my new cologne.

The utter truth is that accepting these more nasty aspects of parenthood is just one of the many new dad tasks you'll have to deal with. Soon, you'll find yourself consumed by washing and sterilizing bottles, feeding, burping, and soothing your baby and obsessing over the color, consistency, and frequency of your baby's poop. Yes, my fellow dads, you'll change more diapers than you could imagine. Just in the first year, babies go through about 2,200 diapers (*How Many Diapers Do I Need for a Newborn?* 2020). You could either see this as 2,200 times you'll have to do this monotonous task, or as 2,200 opportunities to shine as a new dad.

Let's dive into some of the everyday tasks every new dad has to do, including diapering, tummy time, soothing your crying baby, helping your baby adopt healthy sleeping patterns, and why creating a routine could save you and your new family from the chaos that parenthood can bring.

DIAPERING BASICS: FROM CHOOSING THE RIGHT DIAPER TO TACKLING DIAPER RASH

From the day you find out you're going to become a dad, you know that you'll have one of the biggest jobs of your life coming your way: changing diapers. I have to be honest with you. This was probably the part of fatherhood that I was least looking forward to. I struggled to even imagine myself doing it but I realized that I didn't have a choice. On some days this wasn't a pretty picture. It took me a few pee shots in the face to realize that I should always keep my son's business closed with either the diaper or a wet wipe to avoid his fountain spraying in all directions. And when messes landed on me, I tried my best to imagine it was some moldy chocolate to avoid hurling all the way to the bathroom (I have a pretty weak stomach).

Just like I could turn myself into a diaper-changing master, you can as well. Let's first look at the very basics of diapering. Before you even attempt to change the diaper, make sure you have all the necessary supplies within reach. The last the you want is to leave your baby alone on the changing table while you get something or carry your half-naked baby around with you and turn your arm into a porter potty. We always kept extra diapers, wet wipes, bum cream, rash cream, and a change in clothing on the changing table.

To change a diaper, simply open it, gently lift your baby's butt, and use a wet wipe, cotton ball, or washcloth to wipe them clean from the front to the back. This is to reduce the spread of bacteria which could easily result in urinary tract infections, particularly in girls. Once your baby is clean, you can place the new diaper and apply either bum cream (to provide a barrier to protect their skin) or rash cream if your baby has a rash. Always wash your hands before and after changing their nappy.

I have to pause here and share a crucial tip that will save you a lot of time, wet wipes, and elbow grease. Your baby's first few poops, called meconium, will be black and extremely sticky. You'll easily use a whole packet of wet wipes to clean it off their skin or destroy a washcloth so badly that you'll have to throw it away. This meconium typically passes within a few days. To avoid struggling to clean the meconium, apply petroleum jelly to their skin instead of the normal bum cream. The meconium then sticks to the jelly and not their skin, making it easy to just wipe clean. Once the meconium has passed, you can use the barrier cream of your choice.

Soon, you'll become the ultimate king at diapering. It's estimated that an average baby uses around 3,000 diapers only in the first year. If you use disposable diapers, this can easily cost you anything from $1,000 to $3,000 a year, depending on the brand you choose to use (Tech Team, 2023). If you factor in the cost of wet wipes and bum cream, caring for your newborn's bottom can really break the bank.

The cost of disposable diapers as well as the impact they have on the environment are two of the main reasons many people opt for cloth diapers. You can get really nice sets of cloth diapers for between $500 to $1,000 which you'll be able to use throughout your diapering journey and reuse should you have another child (Tech Team, 2023). Yes, you'll still have the expense of wet wipes (unless you only use a washcloth) and bum cream, as well as cleaning products for when you wash the diaper. All of this can add up to quite a substantial expense to have upfront. However, if you look at the bigger picture, you will save money if you use cloth diapers.

Dealing With Diaper Rash

Regardless of the type of diaper you use, there will likely come a time when you'll have to deal with a diaper rash. This is a form of dermatitis on the baby's bottom, inner thighs, and genitals that looks red, inflamed, bumpy, itchy, and sore. While there may be many causes for diaper rash, the most common ones include:

- Leaving a diaper that's wet or soiled on for too long.
- Using a diaper that's too small or too tight can result in their skin getting irritated from chaffing and rubbing.
- Applying a new product to your baby's skin or on their clothes, particularly if the product is scented.
- Developing a yeast or bacterial infection which can easily spread in the diaper area that's often warm and moist.
- Introducing new types of foods once your baby starts eating solids results in changes to their stool contents, which can cause rashes when in context with their skin. A breastfed baby can also get a rash from something the mother has consumed.

- Having sensitive skin, particularly if the baby has a dermatological condition, such as atopic dermatitis or seborrheic dermatitis.
- Taking antibiotics can kill the bacteria that control yeast, which can result in an increased risk of rashes.

In most cases, diaper rashes can be treated fairly easily using a topical cream. However, if it hasn't improved after a few days, is accompanied by a rash, bleeds, or oozes, or if your baby is in a lot of pain or discomfort because of it, it's best to consult a health care professional. A doctor will be able to eliminate any dermatological conditions that might have resulted in the rash and prescribe medicine or ointment to treat the rash.

While it may be inevitable that your child may develop a diaper rash at some point, there are many things you can do to prevent it:

- Change their diaper frequently and as soon as you can after they soiled it. If your child is in daycare, it would be smart to ask the staff to change their diaper more frequently.
- Rinse your baby's bum with warm water at every diaper change. While wet wipes and a washcloth can help to clean their bums, this may cause pain when you wipe over their irritated and inflamed skin. Gently pat dry their skin or let them air dry.
- Make sure you don't secure the diaper too tightly. Slight airflow between the diaper and the skin can help to reduce any irritation in the area.

- Give your baby a few hours without a diaper on. Exposing their sensitive skin to air can help to dry properly. If you're scared your baby will make a toileting mess while they are diaper-free, you can put them on a large towel for a safe home base.
- Always make sure you use enough bum or barrier cream after every diaper change to make sure their skin is protected. There are also many creams you can buy over the counter to treat a diaper rash. Alternatively, you can try these natural remedies:

  ○ Apply coconut oil straight to your baby's clean, dry skin after every use. Coconuts have antimicrobial properties which can not only help to heal a wound but also act as barrier protection.
  ○ If your partner is breastfeeding, you can drop some breast milk straight onto the inflamed skin of your child. Allow the area to dry before you put their diaper back on.
  ○ Diaper creams with zinc oxide or olive oil can be extremely effective in treating irritations to the skin, as these natural ingredients aid in reducing the burn in the skin. These types of creams can be used on any skin type, including very sensitive skin.

Perhaps most importantly, always keep an open mind when you're diapering. I will never forget the day when my baby made such a big explosion in his diaper that I never thought I would be able to clean the mess (or get the smell out of my nose). To make matters worse, I was holding him when the poop started leaking out of his diaper, resulting in my arm and chest getting soaked as well. While I was wiping and wiping to get it all cleaned (I eventually resorted to putting us both in the bath), I burst out in laughter. I could either find the funny in the situation, or I could sit in a smelly heap of self-pity. I chose to find the humor.

THE MAGIC OF TUMMY TIME

During the first few weeks, your newborn will only be awake for a few minutes at a time in between naps. These will mostly be spent feeding, burping, diapering, and then soothing your baby before they fall asleep again. Soon, this will change. Over the following few weeks, they will be awake for longer periods of time and start to engage more, not just with you but with toys as well. Now would be time for the introduction of tummy time.

Tummy time simply refers to placing your baby on their stomach when they are awake while keeping a watchful eye to make sure they don't choke on anything or injure themselves. Tummy time holds many benefits for your baby:

- Your baby's back, neck, shoulder, and arm muscles will strengthen, which will help them to sit independently, crawl, or walk over the coming months.
- Your baby will become more coordinated in their movements as their motor skills develop.
- You'll prevent any flat spots at the back of your baby's head, which is a common occurrence in babies who spend most of their time lying on their backs.

Most babies can start tummy time within the first few days of being born. When they are so young, it's best to keep these sessions short as your baby will tire very quickly. It's best to do these sessions during a time when your baby is happy and content. Around three to five minutes at a time will be more than long enough. As they grow, you can push it to slightly longer sessions repeated a few times during the day. These tips can help make tummy time fun and easy for you and your baby:

- Put a soft blanket on the floor.
- Roll a towel up or use a small round pillow. Prop this under your baby's arms to help them into a slightly more upright position and take the strain off their core muscles.
- Put a toy or something with clear patterns in front of them to keep them engaged, or lie on your tummy in front of your baby with your face close to theirs.

It may be best to avoid doing tummy time straight after a feed as your baby might be uncomfortable due to swallowed winds or too sleepy to properly engage in this exercise. While many babies are happy doing tummy time and even enjoy it, others might dislike it and get cranky. If this is the case for your baby, you can make this time more fun by putting them in different positions or bringing more toys to keep them entertained. Also, keeping these sessions short when they are cranky can help ease your baby into it. Let's look at some age-related tips on introducing tummy time for your baby.

Newborn to 6 Weeks

During the first few weeks, you can incorporate these techniques:

- Instead of putting your baby on the floor, you can lie on your back and put your baby's tummy down on your chest. This way, they can clearly see your face and hear your voice when they lift their little heads.
- Let your baby lie tummy down on your two forearms and walk them through the house.
- Using black and white patterns can help to keep your baby engaged as their limited eyesight can clearly differentiate between dark and light. It's best to keep these patterns 8–12 inches away from their face so that they can clearly see them.
- Place your baby down on their tummy on a yoga or birthing ball. The movement on this ball can help to soothe them if they are cranky or don't enjoy tummy time. Just always make sure that you keep the ball steady and hold your baby the whole time they are on the ball to make sure they don't slip off.

6 to 12 weeks

Once they are getting comfortable with tummy time, you can transition these sessions using the below techniques:

- Experiment with different textures. You can either put your baby down on a textured blanket or use different materials to entertain your baby by gently wiping over their face. This can also help to distract them if they don't enjoy tummy time.

- Place wrist rattles around your baby's arms, and gently put their arms out in front of them. The noise of the rattles will keep their attention in front, which will help them into the optimal position to gain the maximum benefits out of tummy time.
- Hold out a rattle in front of them and shake it until your baby focuses on it. Then, slowly move the rattle around to let your baby's gaze follow the toy. As they get older, your baby will try to grab the toy (speaking from experience).
- Baby gyms can be a great tool to use during tummy time as there will be different colors to look at, music to keep them engaged, and textures to touch.

3 to 4 Months

As your baby gets stronger, they start to lift and keep their heads up by themselves, you can incorporate these techniques:

- Water mats can be a great tool to use during tummy time. These mats are soft for your baby to lie on and contain many floating shapes your baby can watch and try to grab.
- Placing a mirror in front of your baby can be another great way of entertaining and distracting them during tummy time. Even if they don't know that they're looking at themselves, they will have a lot of fun with their new "friend" in the mirror.

4 Months and Older

By now, your baby should be able to keep their heads up independently and reach for objects. These techniques can make tummy time fun:

- Place a tray with different objects on the floor in front of them. These objects can include anything from household items such as sponges or wooden spoons to toys and plastic teething necklaces. Just make sure they are all safe for your baby and don't have any small pieces that can be choked on.
- Put a shallow plastic bowl with some water in front of your baby, add a rubber duck and some friends, and you have a makeshift baby bath. Your baby will enjoy playing with their new floaty friends. Expect to be in a splash zone. If you don't want your carpets or floors to get wet, you might want to do this one outside on a warm day or place a waterproof sheet or even a tarp or trash bag underneath your baby.
- Play games with your baby while they are doing tummy time. Peekaboo is always a fantastic option as it can not only help them enjoy this time but also allow them to understand that even when they can't see you, you'll always be there.

As I've mentioned, these tummy time activities can be great in preventing flat spots on your baby's head, which typically happen when they spend a lot of time lying down. While in most cases this isn't a cause of concern and their heads typically return to a normal round shape as they get older, it is still best to prevent it. If their tummy time isn't enough and the shape of their head still looks slightly like they are from an alien movie, you can incorporate these steps:

- Hold your baby upright as much as possible when they are awake.
- Limit the amount of time your baby spends sitting or lying against something.
- Change your baby's sleeping position in their crib frequently. For example, swap the direction of their bodies around.
- Move your baby's crib to a different spot in their room. That way, they will move their heads in different directions when looking around.

If you're ever worried about your baby's progress during tummy time, their upper body strength, or the shape of their head, it's best to speak to their pediatrician. Even though it will be years before they'll deadlift weights, it's best to be aware of any developmental issues sooner rather than later.

SOOTHING TECHNIQUES FOR A FUSSY BABY: SWADDLING, WHITE NOISE, AND MORE

There's nothing as frustrating as when your baby cries and you have no idea what to do to calm them down. Unfortunately, as much as you may be a pro at bonding with your baby and following their prompts, there still may be times when nothing you try helps to stop the tears from rolling down your little one's cheeks. Or perhaps, bonding hasn't gone as well as you hoped and you still haven't gotten the hang of their different cries yet.

When your baby appears inconsolable, I recommend you follow this checklist to try to bring your baby (and your ears) the comfort they desperately seek:

- Is your baby hungry? When last did they feed?
- Is your baby tired? When are they due for another nap?
- Does your baby have a dirty diaper?
- When last did your baby make a poop? What was the consistency like?
- Does your baby have gas?
- Is your baby struggling with cramps?
- Does your baby have a fever or appear to be sick?
- Is your baby dressed appropriately?
- Is your baby over or under-stimulated?

In most instances, ticking off this list will help you solve their struggles. Unfortunately, there are times when none of these reasons are the culprit, and changing their diaper or feeding them just won't stop the seemingly endless supply of tears. My wife and I found these techniques to be helpful; if not to calm our crying baby, then to calm ourselves. These include:

- Newborn babies have no other way to communicate than to cry, so you can and should expect crying. Also, if you try to see the bigger picture and remind yourself that your baby is trying to communicate something important to you. Those crying sounds at 2 in the morning can become more bearable.
- Give your baby a calming massage by rubbing body lotion onto their skin in slow, circular movements. A

warm bath can also help them calm down. Then, spread a swaddling or receiving blanket out so that it forms a diamond shape and fold the top corner in. Lay your baby on the blanket with their head at the folded corner. Either gently cross your baby's arms over their chest or let their arms lie on their sides. Then, wrap the right corner over your baby and tuck it in underneath them. Bring the bottom corner of the blanket over their feet. Lastly, bring the left corner over to complete the swaddle. Always make sure that you wrap them snuggly but never too tight as this can result in hip dislocation or dysplasia.

- Gently rock your baby in your arms, either sitting in a rocking chair or walking up and down with them. If you have a vibrating or rocking chair, these can be very helpful to soothe a crying baby. Many babies are also comforted by the vibration of a moving car, so if all else fails, strap your baby in their car seat, take them for a ride, and pick up drive-through takeout while on the road. Your partner will be happy for the break, especially when neither of you have to cook dinner.

- If none of these tips help, consider getting some help. There will likely be a grandparent, aunt, or uncle who will be more than happy to sit with your baby while you and your partner have a quick break. Perhaps, they may even bring a new approach to soothing your little one that you haven't tried yet. Even just a few hours away from your little one can be enough to revive you for your next daddy duty shift.

- Should you not have anyone you trust to look after your baby for a few minutes, make sure your baby is placed in a safe environment, such as in their crib or stroller, and leave the room for a few minutes, even if it's just to have a sip of water or make yourself a cup of coffee.
- Before your partner gave birth, or perhaps even during labor, she likely learned some deep breathing exercises to keep her calm. These same breathing exercises can be just as handy when you try to stay calm while your baby is crying. When you hold your baby while you do these deep breathing techniques, they may even pick up on your lowering heart rate.
- If you keep your physical body as healthy as possible, your emotional strength will also improve, which will help you to stay calm. I know it may sound like an old wives' tale to sleep when your baby is sleeping but if it's at all possible (which might be difficult if you're working), try to nap as much as you can during the day. Also, try your best to eat healthy meals. While takeout or processed meals that you only need to heat up may be the easiest and quickest options, healthy meals will help to improve your emotional health.
- You may be hesitant to venture out of the house when your baby is difficult to soothe. However, if you imprison yourself in your house, your frustration levels will likely rise, especially if you're used to having an active social life. Yes, it may be uncomfortable being out and about while your baby is crying and you may even get a few unpleasant

looks, but get over this and enjoy the fresh air outside of your home as both of you will benefit.

- The more time you spend with your baby, the more you'll be able to anticipate their needs and pinpoint times in the day when they might be more cranky. This can help you to prepare and deal with their crying more effectively.

Always remember the bigger picture. Right now, you might struggle to see the light outside this crying tunnel but this crying phase won't last forever.

NEWBORN SLEEP PATTERNS: UNDERSTANDING AND ADAPTING

The first few weeks of having a newborn can be rough on a person. While you love that little human you've created with all your heart, caring for them can be exhausting, to say the least. You'll wake up every few hours to feed your baby, burp them, change their diaper, and then help them to fall back asleep. Especially if your baby is breastfeeding and needs to nurse every two hours, you'll just start to fall asleep again before it's time for the next feed. If you're back at work, this can make it difficult to focus. If your partner is alone at home with the baby all day or perhaps also back at work, she will be equally as tired and in need of your help.

You likely can't wait for the day your baby will sleep through the night. For some lucky parents, this can happen as soon as around the six-week mark, whereas for others, it can be months. We had those opposites in our home. Our first baby was just over six weeks old when he started sleeping through the night. We thought we were parents extraordinaire, which gave us confidence for having a second baby. Unfortunately, sleeping luck wasn't on our side the second time around, as this baby only started to sleep through the night at the age of around three years. As bad as it sounds, you do surprisingly get used to not sleeping properly and find ways to cope.

Since every child's sleeping habits can be vastly different, it can be difficult to know what to expect or what is typical for their specific age. Let's look at the typical sleeping needs of a baby over the first year (Pacheco & Wright, 2023):

First 4 months: Newborns typically sleep anywhere between 16 to 19 hours every day. As we've mentioned, this will unfortunately be broken up into short cycles of sleep in between nursing and diaper changes. Since young babies' blood sugar can drop quickly if they don't feed often enough, you'll need to wake them up if they're still sleeping by the time they are due for their next feed. If they gain an acceptable amount of weight by the time they are six weeks old, their pediatrician may give you the green light to leave your little one for longer periods during the night.

Months 4 to 6: During these months, your baby will need between 12 to 16 hours of sleep at a time. They will be able to go longer between feeds, so their sleep will be clustered into longer sleeping cycles. This can mean they'll have between two to three good naps during the day.

Months 6 to 12: Once your baby passes the six-month mark, they should do most of their sleeping during the night. However, there will still be times when they don't sleep well, particularly when they go through growth spurts or are teething.

Always remember every baby develops differently, and so will their sleeping habits. Use the above simply as a guideline and should you ever be in doubt, discuss this with your baby's doctor.

Even if you have your baby on a strict routine (this can help with improving their sleep cycles), you should keep an eye out for their typical sleep cues and when they appear to be tired. Even if it isn't time for a nap, you should consider listening to your baby's needs. These typical sleeping cues can include yawning, rubbing their eyes, fussing, and crying.

Many babies confuse their nights and days. They'll sleep soundly during the day but struggle to settle at night when you desperately want to get some sleep. If you want to create good sleeping habits and create a healthy circadian rhythm (our body's internal clock that regulates time for sleep and alertness), it's best to first make sure they are stimulated during the day and get plenty of daylight. When you need to change or feed them at night, keep the room as dark as you can. Additionally, try to also make their room darker during the day when they need to nap. Over time, they will associate darkness with sleep, which will help you a great deal in also getting some rest.

You can also create good habits to help them settle at night. Some of these habits we introduced include:

- Bathing the baby at night.
- Changing them into their pajamas.

- Putting on a fresh diaper.
- Reading them a story.
- Singing a lullaby.
- Giving them a nighttime feed as late as you can.
- Dimming the lights.
- Making sure the thermostat is at a comfortable temperature.
- Creating a quiet environment.
- Gently rocking them to sleep or putting them in their crib to settle.

If you want to cuddle them while they fall asleep, you can consider rocking and holding them until they are almost asleep before you put them in their crib. Gradually aim at putting them in their crib while they are less sleepy. This way they'll get used to being in their crib and falling asleep, as well as settling themselves back to sleep when they wake up in the night.

Always place your baby on their backs when you put them to sleep as this reduces the risk of sudden infant death syndrome, a condition where babies die in their sleep without any specific reason. If you ever worry about your baby's sleeping habits or if they continue to wake up often during the night despite your continuous efforts to create a healthy circadian rhythm, you may want to discuss this with their pediatrician or even get the help of a sleeping expert. They might give suggestions on things to try or their doctor may prescribe melatonin pills that you can crush and put in your baby's nighttime bottle to help them settle into a healthy sleeping routine. Always consult your pediatrician before you give your baby any medication as some can be extremely harmful, especially within the first three months.

CREATING ROUTINES FOR YOU AND YOUR BABY

Now, let's take a look at the impact of a routine. When my wife first suggested that we create a routine for our baby, I was severely opposed to it. I didn't like the idea of a schedule telling me when I should do something or raising my child on one. However, as the saying goes, "happy wife, happy life." A few hours later we had a full-on schedule and a few weeks later, I was hooked. We kept the schedule fairly basic but included specific times we'd want to bath our son, feed him, and put him to bed. This not only helped us to adapt to our roles but the predictability also helped my son to settle at night when it was time for bed. However, we did remain flexible on days when our baby was difficult. Life happens, especially with a newborn, and it's important to allow you and your partner some flexibility when it does.

If you want to create your own schedule, you should consider your child's feeding times and adjust their routine as they're able to go longer between feeds. We found it's best to start by working around what they are currently happy with when it comes to eating, sleeping, and alert times. Take a few days and make notes of these times so that you can better understand your baby's patterns, which can be helpful in creating a routine.

When you decide to alter their existing routine, it's best to do this gradually so that you don't suddenly spring big changes on them. For example, if you'd like your baby to nap, you can put them down in their crib a little later and increase this daily until you've stretched them to the new nap time. You essentially need to wean your baby into the routine. Also, be mindful that growth spurts can mess with even the best schedules. Your baby may suddenly not want to sleep even though they've been following the same routine for weeks, or they might want to feed a lot more. While following a routine is helpful, you should always be flexible and just hang in there.

You should adjust your baby's schedule as they grow older. Their sleeping and feeding needs will change, particularly when they start eating solids at around six months. They will also spend a lot more time awake and by the time they reach their first birthday, they might only need one or two naps a day.

TEST YOUR NEW DAD IQ: CHAPTER 4

Becoming a master of the various parenting tasks will require you to do the same thing over and over. Just like from the *Karate Kid*: wax on, wax off. Repetition builds discipline and, therefore, builds habits. Eventually, you will get the hang of it and change diapers without giving it any thought. With this in mind, let's do a quick check to test your new dad's IQ. If you struggle with any of these questions, refer back to the various sections in the chapter to refresh your memory.

1. How long should you wait before you start your baby with tummy time?
2. How can you prevent diaper rashes?
3. Why is swaddling soothing for your baby?

4. How can a routine help you and your baby settle into your new life?
5. When your baby has a diaper explosion, should you take them outside and hose them down to clean?

You're now equipped to tackle daily tasks with what I like to call "rockin' dad energy." Yes, you might cringe at my dad joke here, but guess what, you'll soon be whipping out these dad jokes all the time! It's equally important to be prepared for unexpected health concerns. In our next chapter, we delve deep into navigating complex health issues, ensuring your baby is always in the safest hands: yours.

CHAPTER FIVE
NEWBORN HEALTH GUIDE FOR DADS

Having a sick baby or one with serious health issues is most likely every parent's worst nightmare. I know it was definitely mine. My wife had to stop me from rushing to the doctor whenever my newborn just sneezed. My biggest fear was always febrile convulsions, or fever fits, as most people call it. Unfortunately, that fear became a reality for us.

My son was a few weeks short of his first birthday when my wife got a call from his daycare. They said he didn't look sick and had no fever but something seemed off. He just wasn't his usual, happy self. After fetching him, I insisted that my wife take him to the pediatrician for a checkup, just in case. Apart from a slight rash on his tummy (that only the doctor could see, not us) that we should keep an eye on, the doctor couldn't find any cause for concern.

Just over an hour after getting home, my son started a slight fever. We immediately gave him medication (paracetamol or ibuprofen) to try to break the fever but it didn't work. His fever continued to climb and did so extremely quickly. I started to undress our baby to try to cool him down while we were discussing whether we should go to the emergency room and give it a few more minutes. In the middle of talking about it, suddenly, my son's entire body began to shake. He was having a seizure.

The seizure lasted for less than a minute, although it felt like hours. When it was over, we immediately loaded him in the car and rushed him to the pediatrician. We couldn't believe our eyes when the doctor examined him and we saw the super slight rash from the afternoon, which was now dark red and obvious. The doctor then confirmed that our baby has Roseola —or baby measles—and that febrile convulsions are common due to the rapidly rising fevers that are typical of this disease.

Even though taking our son to the doctor during the afternoon didn't stop his seizure, having gone to the doctor earlier helped the specialist make a diagnosis and start treatment quickly. That day I realized that as parents, and especially new parents, we should always trust our instincts, especially when it comes to the health of our little ones.

To help you navigate your health fears, we'll now look at some of the most common ailments many newborns struggle with, including colic. We'll also discuss whether babies need to take additional vitamins, as well as developmental red flags that should urge you to visit your baby's pediatrician.

COMMON FIRST-MONTH HEALTH CHALLENGES

When you're a first-time dad, any form of health issues can seem extremely daunting, no matter how small and insignificant they may actually be. Unless you have medical training, this may be the first time you're responsible for keeping another human being healthy, which in itself, can feel scary. Luckily, many of the common health challenges many newborns face can be treated easily at home.

Cradle Cap

This is the baby version of seborrheic dermatitis, which results in dandruff in adults (Gill, 2023). In babies, this can result in flaky skin on the baby's scalp and ears, but can sometimes spread to the eyebrows, nose, and armpits as well. While it may look terrifying, it's typically harmless and usually goes away by itself, often by the time the baby reaches three months.

You can follow these three steps to treat cradle cap at home:

- Brush your baby's scalp daily to remove loose flakes of skin from their heads. However, never try to pick on it or scrape it off. You can buy a special brush that's made for cradle caps or a new toothbrush with soft bristles can work just as well. If you see your baby's scalp get agitated, you should brush less often.
- After you've brushed their scalp, you should hydrate it. You can use baby oil or a pure plant oil such as olive, coconut, or almond. Pour a small amount of

this oil into your hand and gently massage it into your baby's head, making sure you are extra careful close to their fontanelle, the soft spot on the top of their head. Let the oil soak for a few minutes and wash it off with a fragrance-free baby shampoo.

- If these steps aren't effective, you can ask your doctor to prescribe a cream. They may opt for either an anti-fungal, zinc, or hydrocortisone cream.

Eczema

This skin condition, also known as atopic dermatitis, can affect people of all ages, including newborns. When this happens, the skin will appear chapped. On light skin tones, it can present as red, brown, or purple, and gray on darker skin. Your pediatrician can prescribe a cream to use, or you can try one of these natural remedies:

- Aloe vera gel is regarded as safe to use on an infant's skin and due to its antibacterial and antimicrobial properties, it can soothe eczema.
- Coconut oil can moisturize the skin, which can help to reduce inflammation and soothe eczema.
- Honey has amazing anti-inflammatory and antibacterial properties and can not only help prevent infections in the skin but also speed up healing.

Jaundice

This happens when there is an excess of bilirubin, which is the yellow pigment that can be found in red blood cells. It results in a yellow discoloration of the baby's eyes and skin. It typically happens in babies born prematurely or whose liver hasn't matured enough yet. In most instances of jaundice, babies don't require specialized treatment. However, in severe cases, it can result in brain damage, so it's always best to get an expert medical opinion.

To test if your baby has jaundice, press gently with your finger on your baby's nose or forehead. If the skin changes to a yellow color before returning to its natural color, they may have jaundice. Unless the jaundice is severe, ensuring your baby is exposed to sunlight is usually effective in treating the condition. Dress your baby in only a diaper and sit with them in a sunny spot in your home, ideally with lace curtains drawn to ensure they don't get too hot or sunburnt.

Baby Acne

This results in small pimple-like bumps on your baby's skin, particularly on their face, neck, and back. They are typically caused by an excess of the mom's hormones that are still in the baby's body after the birth. Although they might not look nice, they will typically clear within the first month or two and very seldom leave any scarring.

Although they don't require any treatment, using aqueous cream instead of soap when you bath the baby can help to moisturize the skin and reduce the appearance of these bumps. Unless the bumps become severe or cause your baby discomfort, you shouldn't need to take them to the doctor for baby acne.

Ear Infection

Earache and infections in a baby can be challenging to deal with, particularly since your baby can't tell you that their ears are sore. Your baby will likely cry a lot, particularly when they are feeding or lying down, and their pain might be worse at night. Older babies may move their hands toward their ears. You can test if your baby has earache by gently pressing the tragus of the ear (the triangular piece in the front of the external ear) back to close the ear opening. If your baby's cries intensify as you do this, you can know that their ears are sore.

Since the aches can be caused by an infection, either viral or bacterial, it's best to take your baby to the doctor as they might need antibiotic ear drops to clear the infection. Until the pain subsides, you should take extra caution when you bathe them to keep their ears dry. You can also hold your baby at a slightly upward angle when you feed them.

Reflux

Reflux typically starts within the first few weeks after the baby is born and is usually the result of an underdeveloped esophagus, which causes the milk they drink to push back up. Babies with reflux will bring the milk up either during or shortly after feeding, hiccup during feeds, cry more during and after feeds, and gulp after burping. It may be that your baby shows all the signs of reflux without the typical spit-up or vomit. If this is the case, your baby may have silent reflux.

If you suspect your baby has reflux, it's best to consult their doctor as there are medications you can give to ease their discomfort. If your baby is formula-fed, the doctor might recommend you swap to an anti-reflux milk or even add a special powder to their milk to make it thicker. You can also burp your baby more frequently and for longer after feeds, and keep them upright for a while after burping them. It can help to give your baby smaller bottles of milk more often.

Fevers

It's highly unlikely that you won't ever have to deal with fevers during your parenting journey. Your baby will have a fever if their core temperature rises above 100.4 °F (Pitone, 2022). As scary as fevers may be, they are signs that your baby's body is trying to fight off an infection and unless these fevers reach dangerously high levels or rise rapidly (as was the case with my baby when he got the seizure) they shouldn't necessarily be viewed in a negative light.

Apart from infections, fevers can also be caused by immunizations and even dressing your baby too warm when it's hot out. Teething can also raise a baby's body temperature but should never go higher than 100 °F (Pitone, 2022).

Paracetamol and ibuprofen can be very effective in lowering a fever. However, you shouldn't give a young baby these medicines without checking with their doctor first. You can also lower their body temperature by removing a layer of their clothes and using a lukewarm facecloth to cool them down. Many people recommend a lukewarm sponge bath as well. Even though this can be very effective, it can cause your baby to shiver and be highly uncomfortable. When your baby has a fever, it's important to make sure they stay hydrated as it can result in your baby losing fluids faster than usual.

If your baby's fontanelles are ever sunken in or building outward, or if they vomit repeatedly, struggle to wake up, have purple spots on their skin, bluish lips, tongue, or nails, or get seizures, it's best to take your baby to the emergency room immediately.

Oral Thrush

This yeast infection is another condition that's very common among babies as they lack the immune system to fight off the excess yeast in their bodies. As the name suggests, the signs of oral thrush will all be in and around their mouth: They may have cracks in the corner of their mouths or cottage cheese-like patches on the tongue, lips, or the insides of their cheeks. While most babies won't experience any discomfort, others may struggle to feed well.

In many cases, the infection will go away by itself within a week or two. However, if your baby is struggling to feed, their doctor may recommend an anti-fungal solution to use in the affected areas. You can also take steps to prevent oral thrush in your baby. This will depend on how you feed them:

- **Formula**: Make sure you clean the bottle teats thoroughly by using hot water, and dish soap. Then, sterilize them to make sure you remove any yeast or bacteria. If you prepare the bottles in advance, you should store them in the fridge to prevent yeast from growing in them. If your baby uses a pacifier, you should take these same steps to clean it.

- **Breast**: If your partner's nipples are red or sore, she might have thrush there, which she can pass onto the baby. There are many anti-fungal creams available that she can apply to her breasts to kill the yeast buildup.

SURVIVING THE TERROR THAT COLIC CAN BRING

I have the utmost respect and sympathy for parents of babies with colic. Imagine your baby crying every day for hours on end and absolutely nothing you do can calm them. You go through your checklist to try to find the cause of their unhappiness, you swaddle them, you rock them until you have no feeling left in your arms, you even take them for hours in your car, but their crying just won't end.

Eventually, you take them to the doctor, because surely there must be something wrong with your little one to cause this extreme level of unhappiness. But, after a thorough examination, the doctor says the words you've been fearing: You are the unlucky winner of a baby with colic. The good news is that colic won't last forever. But, the bad news is that it can take up to six months for the colic to gradually go away.

If you're wondering what colic is or what causes colic, you're not alone. Despite extensive research done on the condition, no one has found conclusive reasons why perfectly healthy babies would have these crying spells. A baby is usually considered to have colic when a baby cries for more than three hours a day, for three or more days a week. These crying spells typically happen at the same time of the day, most often in the early evening.

Unfortunately, there isn't a lot you can do to soothe a baby with colic. You can go through the checklist for soothing your crying baby (as discussed in Chapter 4) just to always make sure there isn't an actual reason for them crying. If none of your usual tricks help to soothe your baby, your main focus should be on trying to keep yourself calm. If you can't handle it anymore, put your baby in a safe spot, such as their crib, while you take a few minute's break. Just make sure there are no loose blankets of stuffed animals that can pose a choking or suffocation risk for your little one.

WHICH VITAMINS YOUR BABY MAY NEED

You may wonder whether your baby needs to get additional vitamins to help boost their health. The answer to this question largely depends on the type of milk you choose to feed your baby. While breastmilk is a rich source of nutrients, vitamins, and minerals, it may lack two important nutrients: vitamin D and Iron. However, this will largely depend on the mother's diet while she is breastfeeding and how many foods rich in these nutrients she eats, plus how many her body absorbs before it's passed to her milk.

Vitamin D is predominantly absorbed through sunlight, so if you're worried that your baby isn't getting enough of this vitamin, you can let them lie in the sun for a few minutes a day. Just make sure you have lace curtains to block out harmful rays and avoid their sensitive skin getting sunburnt. You can also get a liquid vitamin D supplement at your local pharmacy that's safe to give to a baby over the age of three months. Many of these supplements are also rich in vitamins A and C, which not only help with the absorption of vitamin D but iron as well.

Iron is important for healthy brain development. If you suspect your breastfed baby has an iron deficiency, your partner can increase the iron-rich foods she eats, such as leafy green vegetables and meat. Alternatively, you can discuss this with your doctor to get recommendations on an iron supplement to give to your baby.

Supplemental vitamins are typically not necessary for babies who are formula-fed, as their formula will already be fortified with sufficient levels of iron, vitamin D, and many other nutrients. It may be helpful to check the content of these vitamins in your child's formula, or if you're alternating between breast milk and formula, you should discuss any concerns with their pediatrician. Once your baby starts solids at around six months, especially if they are a picky eater, it's best to reconsider their vitamin needs again.

Should you opt to give your baby supplemental vitamins, it's best not to mix them in your baby's milk as the calcium in the milk can affect the absorption of the vitamins, particularly iron.

HEALTH RED FLAG CHECKLIST

Every baby develops at their own pace and, as a result, you should always read the various monthly milestones that are available online with a whole bag of salt (a pinch just isn't enough). With all due respect to these references, they often work on the ideal baby's development, which can be very far removed from reality. Let me give you an example: My eldest developed at a textbook pace: He sat independently at six months, crawled at eight months, and walked just before his first birthday. Then, my wife gave birth to our pocket rocket second child who defied all those typical milestones: She sat independently at four months, crawled at six months, and was literally running around the house at nine months (it seemed like she completely skipped past the walking phase).

Because of my experience, I don't believe in lists of milestones babies should reach by specific months. Instead, I want to share a checklist of red flags that might indicate that it may be a good idea to take your baby to their pediatrician for a checkup (*Red Flags by Age for Referral of a Child*, 2021):

1 month:

- Can't follow moving objects with their eyes, even extremely briefly.
- Doesn't startle when they hear a loud noise.

2 months:

- Doesn't respond to loud noises at all.
- Can't hold their head up during tummy time.
- Can't bring their hands to their mouth.

3 months:

- Can't push their chest up during tummy time.
- Don't turn their head in response to movement.
- Doesn't smile at people.
- Don't laugh when you try to entertain them.

4 months:

- Can't support their own head.
- Doesn't make any coos or sounds.
- Struggles to move their eyes in different directions.
- Don't push down with their legs when you put their feet on a hard surface.

6 months:

- Doesn't reach for things.
- Doesn't respond to sounds.
- Doesn't seem sturdy, almost like a rag doll, or extremely stiff.
- Can't roll over when lying on their backs.
- Shows no affection for others, particularly their primary caregivers.
- Doesn't make sounds, especially vowel sounds.

9 months:

- Can't bear weight on their legs with support.
- Can't sit, even with help.
- Doesn't respond to their own name.
- Can't recognize familiar faces.
- Can't transfer toys from one hand to the other.

- Doesn't look where you're pointing.

12 months:

- Doesn't crawl.
- Doesn't stand with support.
- Doesn't point to things.
- Don't wave bye-bye.
- Doesn't shake their head when they don't want something.
- Doesn't say a single word.
- Loses skills they used to be able to do.

While these red flags don't necessarily mean that there's something wrong with your baby, it's best to have your little one checked out by the doctor to make sure there isn't a medical reason for their slow development.

TEST YOUR NEW DAD IQ: CHAPTER 5

Having a baby with health concerns can be a major worry for all parents, particularly first-time parents who aren't used to caring for the health of another person. Many of the common ailments many newborns face are luckily not serious. Let's do a quick check to test your new dad's IQ. If you struggle with any of these questions, refer back to the various sections in the chapter to refresh your memory on this very important chapter.

1. How can you treat mild cases of jaundice at home?
2. Is colic a result of a medical condition or illness?

3. If your baby has baby acne, does that mean your child will struggle with pimples throughout their childhood into their teenage years?
4. Why shouldn't you add vitamins to a baby's milk?
5. If you have a colic baby, is it okay to put earplugs in your ears and ignore them for hours at a time?

Now that you're equipped with the knowledge to navigate complex health concerns, the journey doesn't stop there. As a new dad, balancing fatherhood with personal life can be a tightrope walk. In the next chapter, let's explore how to find that equilibrium, ensuring you don't lose sight of yourself while embracing your new role.

CHAPTER SIX
BALANCING FATHERHOOD
WITH PERSONAL LIFE

I 'll never forget one team-building day I had at work. This was a few months after I became a dad for the second time. My colleagues and I did many different activities together. Some were physical (obstacle courses and such), while others were mental and even emotional.

During one of the more mental challenges, we had to answer a series of questions about ourselves. They were mostly easy ones, such as describing yourself in five words, your favorite food, and your dream vacation spot. Those types of questions. However, one of these questions had me completely stumped. We had to jot down our biggest strengths and weaknesses. One answer for each of them, but we only had five seconds to do so. It was one of those moments where you just write down the first thing that pops into your head. Without any hesitation or even thinking about it, I found myself writing, "my family" for both answers. It was only later after doing some proper self-reflection that I understood why my family is both a strength and a weakness.

The strength part was fairly obvious: They are my biggest driving force for success. Every day, I want to be a better person for my wife and a better father for my baby. I would do anything to protect them. Seeing them happy and thriving is a massive motivator for me. So, why would I then also consider them to be my biggest weakness? Eventually, I understood that it was for the exact same reason: Since they are my main motivators to becoming the best possible version of myself, I felt like I was letting them down when I experienced setbacks or made mistakes. And, since I'm only human, mistakes and challenges are part of my daily life. I felt like I was doomed to fail my family.

My wife could see I was dealing with a lot of inner conflict. One night after the kids were both in bed, we had a long discussion about this. She helped me understand that the deep feelings I have for my family are one of the most beautiful things, even though it makes me feel weak at times. She also reminded me that even though being a father and a husband are the most important roles in my life, I was also a human being.

This whole experience reminded us both of the importance of living a balanced life. You can't be so overly focused on doing right by your family that you neglect yourself. On the flip side of the coin, you also can't become selfish and only do things for yourself. The coin toss between life and fatherhood is all about striking the perfect balance. Unfortunately, I often found it easier to find this balance on a seesaw with my 180-

pound body on one side and my 40-pound son on the other. You can't manipulate the seesaw of life by keeping your weight-bearing feet on the ground as you can on the playground.

I was lucky to have my wife's full support in trying to find this perfect balance. Together, we worked on various strategies to not only find pockets of "me time" during the day for both of us but also to bring the spark back to our relationship and make time for friends. We also decided on implementing strict boundaries, with each other, our extended family, our friends, and work colleagues. I know it sounds like a lot, but I quickly learned communication is key.

REDISCOVERING PERSONAL SPACE: FINDING POCKETS OF "ME TIME"

Being the hands-on father I know you are (or will be), it can be difficult to even imagine taking time for yourself, let alone actually doing it. Let me tell you how my brain would operate, every day before work, I would help get everything ready in the house and for our baby. The same goes for after work: I do my part in the kitchen helping to prepare dinner and clean up afterward. I always tried to make time to play with the baby. Then, I took care of bathing the baby. And my wife and I would alternate putting our little one to sleep. I remember thinking it would be impossible to fit in "me time;" my schedule was just too busy.

However, my wife and I both realized how important it is to remain an individual and not just a parent. To do this, we decided to focus on the quality of the "me time," not the length of time. Because, let's face it, scraping ten minutes for yourself is a lot easier than hoping for a full hour solo. These are some of the strategies we implemented to find these pockets of "me time":

Think or journal about what "me time" means to you: Every person will have their own idea of "me time" and how they want to use it. Consider what you regard as "time well spent" and how you can do more of that in your life. It can be helpful to make a list of different short activities you can try to bring into this time.

Always have a shower: I know this might sound ridiculous but when you're consumed with parenting tasks, making time to clean yourself might not be at the top of your list. But, if you're able to make time for this, you will not only feel better about yourself but also get a few minutes of self-care. If you don't have anyone to watch your baby while you shower, you can put them in a rocking or vibrating chair with you in the bathroom.

Shop while they are sleeping: If you need to do some shopping, try to do it while your baby's sleeping peacefully in their stroller. There is probably nothing worse than having to walk through shops with a crying baby. But, if they are able to sleep sweet and sound, you can enjoy the experience a lot more. The movement of the stroller will likely at the same time help rock them to stay asleep for longer.

Catch up while you feed: While you're feeding your baby, you'll spend a lot of time seated. Why not use this time to relax and binge your favorite show or listen to a podcast while you're feeding your baby? This can, therefore, double as precious "me time" as well.

Use nap times to relax: We often try to rush through our chores while the baby is asleep. When they awake, we are left feeling exhausted by the time they wake up and need our attention again. Create a rule that this time should only be used for relaxing activities. If you do, you'll feel more energized when your baby wakes up. When our children were babies, we made peace with the fact that our house didn't look perfect. We just reminded ourselves that guests came to visit us and see our baby, not to judge us for the state of our house.

See your time as being more valuable than money: While you can always take out a loan if you need extra money, you can't ever do this with time, so think about how you want to spend your time. If you have ten minutes to spare, what would you like to do to get the most out of the time?

Destroy time wasters: We all have little habits that waste our time. This can be playing games on our phones or checking social media every few minutes. If we can identify these time wasters and work to reduce them, we'll potentially gain a lot more time to spend on more relaxing or valuable activities.

Add "me time" to your schedule: One of the best ways of making sure you get time to relax is to schedule it. This way your partner will also be on the same page when you're going to enjoy a few minutes by yourself, which will help her to plan your baby's routine accordingly. Always remember to also add some "me time" for your partner to the schedule so she can also enjoy time by herself to relax.

Be sure that you have realistic expectations when it comes to finding pockets of "me time." You can't expect to suddenly have hours of time to yourself when your partner and baby need you.

STRENGTHENING YOUR RELATIONSHIP: KEEPING THE SPARK ALIVE

As I've mentioned a few times, becoming a parents will change your relationship with your partner. No matter how much you might live in a dream world where becoming parents won't impact your connection, it's just not realistic. Where you could spend as much time alone together as you both wanted to, your days will now revolve around your little one. However, this doesn't have to be negative. In fact, I know many couples who make it through parenting an infant stronger than ever before. Luckily, there are many ways in which you can work on keeping the spark alive in your intimate relationship. These are some of the strategies we implemented:

Discuss your parenting views: If you and your partner are on the same page on how you want to parent your baby, you'll avoid a lot of unnecessary conflict in your relationship. This can also increase the trust you have in your co-parent, as you'll know that any decisions to be made when you're not around will be in alignment. Some hot topics you should discuss can include discipline, education, religion, and access your extended family should have with your baby.

Multi-tasking time: You're likely used to spending a lot of time together as a couple, but this will change when you become a parent. Instead of it just being the two of you, you'll now be a family of three or more. However, having an extra human being around shouldn't mean that you and your partner can't connect. All it takes is to use the time you do have more effectively. How can you two do this? For example, my wife and I would have deep discussions while feeding the baby or even doing chores around the house. We realized that if you're both invested, not just in the relationship but also in the conversation, you don't have to sit still to have a meaningful discussion.

Talk about your finances: There aren't a lot of things that can result in arguments quite like different views on finances. But, if you and your partner are in agreement with how you'll spend your money and have budgets in place, you'll be better prepared for when all the unexpected expenses that a baby can bring come your way. We created a rule where we decided on a set amount of money per month and agreed that before spending a cent more, we'd discuss it first. This helped to increase the trust and appreciation in our relationship.

Look to the future: Another thing you and your partner should continuously be talking about is your hopes and dreams for the future. This will be extremely valuable if you communicate well. Sharing your future plans will help remind you of everything you have to look forward to. It will give you both hope that you'll survive the chaos that life with a newborn can bring and that you can even get to the other side stronger than ever before.

Connect intimately: Fellas, your eyes probably lit up now thinking that I'm referring to having sex again. Yes, I do believe sex is important in every relationship, it shouldn't be the be-all and end-all of your intimacy with your partner. She has been through a physical and emotional rollercoaster to give you a baby. Even if the six weeks that most doctors recommend new mothers abstain from sex post-birth is over, it doesn't mean your partner will be ready to become sexually active again. Look at other ways of being more intimate with your partner that won't necessarily lead to a happy ending. Hold your partner's hand, massage her back, or cuddle with her on the couch to remain connected. Perhaps, watch a throwback movie to when you first met. Tune into your teenage self and just enjoy the rush that other levels of intimacy can bring.

My new dad friends, I'm not going to lie to you: There were a few times when I thought my marriage wouldn't survive the newborn phases. Now that my children are bigger, I can honestly say our marriage didn't just make it through these challenging times, but we thrived because of them. I am forever grateful to my wife, not just for helping me create our beautiful children but also for being willing to work with me on strengthening our bond. We are a team. And, let me be the first to tell you that I am not perfect. So, the fact that she's willing to practice patience with me too, is a blessing in itself. When we got married, we promised, "Until death do us part." We did everything we could to make sure that doesn't change to, "Until newborn do us part."

INTEGRATING FRIENDS AND SOCIAL LIFE INTO FATHERHOOD

Just as your relationship with your partner will change once you become a parent, your connections with your friends can also suffer due to the demands of fatherhood. I am a complete extrovert and always had large groups of friends. Unfortunately, I only discovered after the birth of our son that they were more "good time" friends than good friends. When I couldn't meet them as much as I used to anymore, their interest in my life seemed to play a disappearing act on me. Or as the kids nowadays call it (including my own), I got "ghosted."

As much as this frustrated me, I decided to focus on my family. For a while, I was so consumed by slotting into my new role that my heavily declining social life didn't bother me as much. However, as my baby grew and I gained a bit more free time, I was desperate for some time with my buddies again. Judging by my wife's encouragement to reconnect with some of my friends, I'm sure she could also do with me getting a boost from some social interaction.

Unfortunately, I had no idea how to restart my social life again. I've never been in a position where I had to reach out to and potentially be rejected by friends. It always came so naturally, so putting myself out there again (first time since high school) was new territory for me. These are some of the steps I took to reach out and regain my social life:

Reconnecting with old buddies: I started by contacting my old friends one by one. I did this over messaging and since I wanted to send personalized messages to them instead of just copying and pasting a mass message, it was quite a time-consuming task. I used my "me time" moments to do this, as well as while feeding my little one. I started these messages by telling them what was happening in my life, how I've survived the newborn phase, and how I missed hanging out. For those friends who were fathers, I added some information on my baby but didn't want to bore the childless friends with an overload of baby pictures. Then, I asked about how they were doing. I resisted the urge to immediately invite them for a quick lunch or game of golf. Instead, I used this time just to check in.

Recall memories: I went through some of my old photos and created a folder on my laptop where I copied some of my best memories with friends. Once this was done, I posted a photo every other day on my social media accounts and tagged them in it. Some of the pics that might have been a bit more "early days college-themed," I forwarded privately to them. This helped to open the conversation of reminiscing together, which eventually led to lines such as, "It would be great to catch up!"

Set up a get-together: Eventually, messages turned into phone calls. Before I knew it, we connected again, and I had a few lunches marked on the calendar. My father took my wife and baby out on a relaxing day, which was a nice bonding for them. It was great knowing that I didn't have to worry about them at home or rush back to help out. I might have been a little nervous beforehand, not going to lie. But, once we met at the lunch spot, it was like no time had passed.

Find a common interest: One of my old friends is a sports freak just like me. His baby is actually only a few months older than my son, so we have a lot of similarities in our lives. Our wives also used to get on like a house on fire. As a result, I thought he would be a fantastic person to form a deeper friendship with. There was a half-marathon coming up in our city in a few months and even though neither of us were runners, I saw this as a golden opportunity. After convincing him to enter the race with me, we started training together. This didn't mean that we would go for runs every day; our schedules didn't allow for this. Instead, we mostly trained separately in our own time but would share our training performances with each other. This common goal was a fantastic re-entry point to what is now one of my best friendships.

Connect while you're at home: Another friend of mine is big into gaming. I've never really been a gamer, but I had an Xbox at home. I saw on Facebook that he really enjoys a specific game, so I asked him more about it. Eventually, he offered to help me get started. We connected our Xboxes and played together online. I did this while my son was happily playing with his toys right next to me. I'll admit, I didn't become a full-on gamer like some of those YouTubers, but I now can play a mean game of FIFA.

Join online groups: While I was posting photos on Facebook, I wondered if there weren't any first-time dad groups I could join. I mean, there are groups for literally everything on Facebook. After a quick search, I joined a few groups. What a great idea that was! I could connect with other first-time dads from the comfort of my child's play mat. Not only did I learn many hacks on these groups, but it was also great to know that other first-time dads also wondered why their babies would play with a dead worm that they had found in the grass. It was fantastic to know we weren't quite as odd as I started to suspect.

Apart from these tips, I also learned to forgive and forget small things that happened in the past. There was no reason for me to still be upset over an old friend who got the girl I was after 15 years ago. I should actually thank him because if he didn't also pursue her, I might never have met my wife. Giving up past hurts and arguments made me more susceptible to new friendships.

SETTING BOUNDARIES: NAVIGATING ADVICE AND RELATIVES

As I worked on expanding our circle of friends, I became more and more aware of the need to have proper boundaries in place to protect myself and my new family. These boundaries were not just for my friends but for my relatives as well. I had an aunt who would just pop by unannounced to spend time with the baby. As much as we appreciated the love she had for him, I can't tell you how many times I had to run to the room to get dressed suddenly while she was standing at our front door. Because, yes, my fellow new dads, there are many Saturday mornings that I sit in the living room wearing only my boxers.

Healthy boundaries are all about making sure you only allow things to enter your life that you're truly comfortable with. Doing the sprints in my underwear to the room while my aunt was in the house wasn't something that would fall in my comfort zone. I had to sit my aunt down and explain to her that as much as we love her presence in our lives and appreciate the love she showed our son, she needed to communicate to us when she wanted to visit and not just show up. At first, I could see she took offense as she believed a person shouldn't have to create a formal meeting to see family, let alone her nephew. But, she saw I wasn't budging on the boundary, so she had to comply.

This is just one example of the many boundaries we created to make our lives easier and to protect us from unwanted (or embarrassing) situations. I urge you to think about your life and make a list of the things you're either uncomfortable with or absolutely don't want in your life. Remember, this is your life so even if you feel it may be selfish, don't ignore your feelings. The person you're creating the boundary for will rarely be happy with the limitations you're setting, so make peace with that and do what's right for you and your family.

Once you have your list of the unwanted behaviors or circumstances you want to avoid, think about the boundary you want to set. What changed behaviors or circumstances would you be willing to accept? What boundaries can be set to enforce this? Also, since the other person will likely object to these, decide beforehand which of your new limits are non-negotiables, and how far you're willing to compromise on the others.

After you've created your list of boundaries, you need to discuss these with the other people involved. Explain to them honestly why you can't allow their behavior to continue and what you expect from them going forward. Remember that you can't expect these people to smell that you've created a boundary, as if a boundary needs to be set, clearly there is a disconnect to begin with there. If you don't tell them, they'll never know that they should change their behavior. If you're discussing a boundary that is non-negotiable. Where you are willing to compromise, listen to them, give your feedback, and see how you can decide on a way forward together. If you need time to think after listening to their point of view, explain that so you can problem-solve with them.

You can follow these steps in any situation, from setting boundaries with your partner, your child (when they are older), your family and friends, and even your boss or work colleagues. Always remember you have the right to stand up for yourself and what you want in your life. Don't be the fool that I was that had to run around the house in your undies unless that's something you enjoy, of course!

TEST YOUR NEW DAD IQ: CHAPTER 6

Finding the balance in your new life can be tricky, especially if you're still getting used to your role as a first-time dad. But, let me tell you, once you're able to navigate the seesaw without needing to put your feet on the ground for support, you'll find so much more enjoyment in life than you might have thought possible. Before we move on to the final chapter, let's do a quick check to test your new dad's IQ. If you struggle with any of these questions, refer back to the various sections in the chapter to refresh your memory.

1. Why is it important that you and your partner are on the same page in terms of parenting values?
2. Can I set boundaries without communicating with the other person?
3. Once your partner reaches the big six-week postpartum milestone, is it okay to expect her to resume intimacy?
4. If you've lost contact with many of your old friends during the newborn stage, should you just give up on having friends again?
5. Do you need hours by yourself for "me time?"

While balancing the new and old parts of your life, there's another essential aspect we mustn't forget: Capturing the fleeting moments of your baby's growth. In the next chapter, dive deep into the world of documenting milestones and creating beautiful memories to cherish forever. We'll also cast our gaze further and discuss what lies beyond these initial 365 days of your baby's life.

CHAPTER SEVEN

DOCUMENTING MILESTONES AND LOOKING AHEAD

Y ou've probably heard the famous saying that even though the days are long, the years can be short many times before. Never have I found this to be as true and applicable as in parenthood. There are days when you literally want to run for the hills to escape. First from your newborn's cries, then your toddler's tantrums, your elementary school's principal, and finally, your teenager's mood swings. Trust me, fellas, it doesn't always get easier as your child grows up.

However, just as long as your days can sometimes feel, so short are the years. I remember many people telling me to appreciate every second of fatherhood as they grow up so quickly, but I never truly understood how quickly the years would fly by. It feels like I blinked and my firstborn son was ready for school.

Even though you make memories every day in raising your child, you won't remember half of them. These amazing times that should make fantastic memories come so quickly and fast that it can honestly be difficult to keep track of all of them. My wife was good at always keeping her phone with her and capturing as many memories as she could. She took amazing photos and videos of me playing with our little one. Unfortunately, since she was always behind the lens, I never even thought of taking photos of her with our son. I wasn't earning an Oscar for my director skills.

To try to help get you in the running for this imaginary award, we'll now discuss the importance of capturing memories (and making sure your partner also features in these photos). I'll also give you tips a photographer friend of mine gave me when I tried to rectify my mistakes with our second child. These tips will help take your photos from "meh" to "blow up and put on the wall" art pieces, even if you're only using your phone's camera.

We'll also look beyond the first year to the terror that can come with toddlerhood. Fear not, every stage comes with breathtakingly joyful moments.

THE IMPORTANCE OF CAPTURING FIRSTS

Take a moment to think of your favorite memories on your parenting journey so far. Allow me to take a guess: Depending on where you are on your journey, these memories most likely include the day you found out your partner was pregnant, the day you first heard your baby's heartbeat on an ultrasound scan, definitely the day your little one was born, and perhaps already a few others.

When we are emotional, our memories are processed differently in our brains—neurons in the amygdala activate during emotional responses—making them more clear and longer lasting. These can be positive and negative feelings, which is why traumatic experiences can be just as vivid in your memory as positive ones. When you find a reminder of a positive experience, such as a photo of one of your baby's first smiles or their belly laughs, it brings back the strong emotions you experienced during that event, which will help you remember that wonderful moment with a lot more clarity.

I experienced this the other day when a friend of mine, who is about to have his first baby, asked me about the birth of our children. I told him as much as I could remember, but to be honest, I was shocked at how vague my memory was. I could recall the big moments but those small things that were so precious to me at the time were rusty in my memory. That night, I took out the old photo albums (my wife prefers to have old-school hardcopy photo albums, not just digital ones) and as I looked through the photos, the memories of those amazing moments flushed back. I felt just as emotional as I did the day I first heard my son's first cries.

My wife and I spent hours looking at the photos and recalling stories. If it wasn't for the photos, so many of those memories would be lost. Again, I was featured like a super dad in those photos, since my wife took most of them. The lack of photos of my wife was so evident that she even joked that it looked like I was a single dad. She thought her joke was very funny. I didn't. I wished I could have a time machine. Fellas, I'll say it again. Learn from my mistakes and take photos of your partner with your baby. She will thank you for it.

TIPS FOR TAKING MEMORABLE PHOTOS

As I've mentioned, after I realized my blunder in not taking photos of my wife with our baby, I really wanted to step it up when our daughter was born. Luckily, I have a very successful photographer friend, Annika. I asked her for some tips on taking the best possible photos using just my cell phone. I really wanted to impress. And, I did. We now have an album filled with photos of my wife, our newborn daughter, and the proud big brother (at the time of writing this book we only had 2 kids to our name, oh how that has changed). In fact, now it looked as if my wife was a single mom.

To help you gain confidence behind the camera to capture beautiful images of your little one, I'll now share Annika's amazing tips:

Go down to their level: Too many pictures of little children are taken from above from your height. Not only do children look fairly awkward (their head is closer to the camera lens, so it naturally seems too big for their body), but they also won't be comfortable. If you bend down to take the picture from the front, their bodies will be proportionate and since you won't stand in front of them as an imposing figure, they will be more at ease. You'll not only get better reactions and facial expressions out of them but you'll also see their faces a lot more clearly in the photos.

Take more than one picture: Camera phones capture images fairly quickly, which makes it easy to take multiple pictures in a single go. If you have an iPhone, you can hold down the button to take batches of photos at lightning speed. Use this to your advantage and take a few pictures from different angles. If you can, move around so that not all the photos are from the front view. Sometimes, side-view photos can be exceptionally powerful. Don't forget about the zoom function when you take these pictures. Your first photo could be the ultimate winner, but you never know what treasures you might capture if you just take a few more.

Grab a bag of patience: Young babies are the perfect photography models as they have no choice but to lie still for as long as you need them to. Toddlers, however, are on the complete opposite side of the scale. They often don't want to sit still, smile, or cooperate in any way. Unfortunately, you'll have to push through and make something work if you want your older child to also feature in photos. Annika is all about taking "candid" photos, not posed ones, which is actually perfect for photographing a toddler. Just sit patiently with your camera ready to capture. When they do something cute, click immediately. Trust me, they move fast so you won't have a lot of time. If you missed the shot, just wait until they either do it again or do something else (perhaps even better than your first try). However, don't ask them to do what they just did again. Trust me, new dads, you'll most likely end up with a tantrum.

Look for natural light: If you are in a room with natural light coming in through a window, place the person you want to take a photo of close to that window. This way the natural light will shine on the person's face, improving the quality of the image drastically. If you want to take photos of a difficult subject (again, think toddler), encourage them to play close to the window while you snap them without them realizing you're taking a photo.

Always look at the background: I'm sure you've seen those photos of someone sitting on a park bench with a massive tree branch growing out of their head. If the person in the photo just moved a few inches to the side, this same branch could've framed them beautifully. When you want to encourage your child to play somewhere with enough natural light, first look at the background. Remember, it's best to move your toddler once to avoid them having a meltdown. If you only realized that there's something in the background and your child isn't in the mood to be moved, consider changing your angle.

There's a dinosaur above my head: Have you ever looked at pictures of young children and wondered why their smiles like so exceptionally fake or even skewed when they usually have the sweetest smile? Annika believes that in most of these cases, the photographer prompted them with the age-old habit, "Say cheese!" Instead of trying to get your child to smile on demand, do something that will make them give a genuine smile or even laugh. You can do faces, make funny sounds, or as worked best with my son, tell them, "There's a dinosaur above my head!" This way, I got him to even look in the camera's direction; double bonus. If these tricks don't work, moody or serious facial expressions can sometimes make even better photos than the typical smiles. Otherwise, just remain ready, armed with your bag full of patience. Eventually, you'll get a real smile out of them.

Take photos in .5: If you're using an iPhone, you can use the .5 setting on your phone to capture more of the setting. It really is a cool hack. If you're using an Android phone, play around with the different options in the phone's camera. You'll be surprised at the amazing photos these little gadgets can take.

Sometimes, even if you follow all these tips, it's just not possible to take that perfect picture you want to hang on your wall. So, I have to share this story with you. While I was in my photography craze after the birth of our daughter in the hopes of scoring serious brownie points, my sister came to visit with her son. He was just over three years old at the time, and if you look up the explanation of the phrase "terrifying toddler" in the dictionary, you'll see a picture of him there. Just joking, of course, but he could throw a meltdown like no other.

I really wanted to get a picture of our children with their cousin, but he just wouldn't cooperate. He kept on screaming something that I honestly couldn't understand. My sister eventually told me to stop trying. He just wouldn't stop crying. After standing dumbfounded for a few minutes, I decided to just go with it. By that time, he knew too well that I tried to take a photo of him, so we ended up with photos of my baby lying there (because she had no choice), my son using her tummy as a track for his little toy car, and the cousin crying in the background. And, you know what, those are now some of our favorite photos and are not just up on the wall in our house, but in my sister's as well.

PREPARING FOR THE TODDLER STAGE

You've likely heard of toddler tantrums before, seen them in the lines at shops, or got scared reading about my nephew above. Unfortunately, once your baby grows into this phase, it's too late to get scared of a little meltdown. Now, you just need to power through. Luckily, it doesn't last very long, but there is a reason why people refer to these ages as the "terrible twos" and "terrifying threes."

These little humans are growing fast and learning to do new things every day. They typically know exactly what they want and their willpower is second to none. Unfortunately, their brain development often lags behind their physical abilities. This can result in them desperately wanting to do something, but lacking the words to explain their wants and needs to you. If you don't immediately know what their disjointed mumbles mean, they get upset. I mean, let's face it, you would also get upset when you believe you explain yourself perfectly to another person, and they just don't seem to understand you.

Their little bodies and brains don't know how to cope with these extremely intense emotions. As a result, they have a meltdown, which can result in uncontrollable crying, throwing their bodies down onto the floor in frustration, or even hurting themselves. Remember, they don't mean to be the terrifying little monsters that they appear to be. They just can't think of better ways of showing you that they are upset.

Luckily, toddlerhood isn't all bad. Not even close to all bad. This is an amazing time when you'll be astounded on a daily basis by the incredible development your child is showing. They'll start to talk in short little sentences. You probably already can't wait to have full-on conversations with your baby. But, be careful what you wish for. On some days, it feels as if my pocket rocket of a daughter tries to say all the words in the dictionary at least six times. There's never a quiet moment with her in the vicinity.

Your child's physical skills will also improve. Soon, your little baby will be running around climbing on everything they see. Yes, my new dad friends, your heart will skip a few beats as you watch your little one try gravity-defying jumps off a jungle gym. Some days I wished those capes my son loved to wear pretending to be Superman, would really turn him into a superhero so that my heart could have a little vacation.

They will slowly but surely become more independent. I won't ever forget the day my wife phoned me while I was still at work. She was so excited that I could barely hear a word she said. Apparently, my son just finished making his own peanut butter and jelly sandwich. It's those little moments in life that turn into the big ones. I must admit, I felt both proud and a little sad when I heard he was such a "big boy" to make his own lunch. My baby boy most definitely wasn't a baby anymore.

The third book in my series, *You Will Rock as a Dad: 85 New Dad Toddler Hacks* The Easy-To-Implement Modern Dad Cheatsheet will uncover everything you need to know about toddlerhood: The good, the bad, and downright ugly tantrums. I will share all the amazing strategies and techniques that helped us survive and thrive through this stage. Together, we can continue our amazing teamwork that helped you rock as a dad during pregnancy and the first year of your baby's life.

TEST YOUR NEW DAD IQ: CHAPTER 7

Time flies when you're having fun, and also when you're raising children. No matter how difficult some days might be, they will soon be a distant memory that you wish you could relive. Yes, chaps, soon you'll even wish you could have those bad days again. That is how amazing fatherhood is. Since no one has successfully invented a time travel machine yet (or at least, not that I know of), you'll have to rely on your memories to reminisce about past milestones. So, let's test your new dad IQ to make sure you capture these moments properly (unlike I did with my firstborn). If you struggle with any of these questions, refer back to the various sections in the chapter to refresh your memory.

1. Why do we remember emotional memories much more clearly?
2. How can you ensure your photos have adequate natural light?
3. What often happens when you tell a young child to "say cheese"?
4. Why is it important to make sure your partner is in many of the photos?
5. If your child doesn't want to sit still for a photo, is it okay to tie them to a chair? (I am absolutely joking. Please don't think I tie my children to chairs!)

As we wrap up this guide, remember that fatherhood isn't just about the destination but the journey. Each chapter of your child's life brings its unique set of challenges and joys. As you've navigated the first year, take a moment to reflect on the beautiful journey ahead.

CONCLUSION

This first year is just the opening chapter to an epic tale of fatherhood. As you've navigated the initial joys and challenges, know that every moment, every stumble, every triumph is shaping you into an even better father. Soon, you'll rock at this little old thing called fatherhood, if you aren't already.

Life with a newborn can be tough on even the emotionally strongest people. But, if you make sure you set the right expectations, learn the power of patience, with your baby and your partner who has just been through thick and thin to bring your child to life, and focus on doing the basics right while focusing on what you can control, you'll get through it with flying colors.

Being a dad doesn't just mean you've impregnated your partner. It means sharing the responsibilities. Those dirty diapers won't clean themselves. Even if you have to swallow your vomit ten times cleaning up a poop explosion or dodging the fountains that boys can make, you can do it. I know you can. Remember, even though breast milk is considered golden milk for your baby, it's more important to just make sure your little one is fed. So, if your partner can't breastfeed, get into problem-solving mode. Formula is an excellent alternative to breast milk. Take charge of certain parenting tasks, and use these moments with your baby as the precious bonding experiences that they can and should be. Remember, bonding isn't just a maternal thing.

Always keep an eye out for any health concerns in your baby. Many of these can easily be treated at home, so if you're ever unsure, refer back to Chapter 5 for tips. But, remember, pediatricians are trained not only in treating illness in babies but also in dealing with terrified first-time parents. So, if you want the reassurance that the pimple on your baby's cheek is only baby acne, don't hesitate to take it. As the saying goes, prevention is always better than cure. Also, refer back to the health red flags we discussed in this chapter and take your baby for a thorough checkup if you're ever concerned about any of them.

Remember to try to find the perfect balance in your life between being a father, a partner, and an individual. When you need to, steal a pocket of "me time," but remember to encourage your partner to do the same. She will most likely also be desperate for some time by herself, even if it's just a few minutes. Never disregard the impact that "New Dad Anxiety" can have, not only in your life but also in the lives of your partner and baby. Having emotions and experiencing anxiety doesn't make you weak. Instead, communicating your feelings and that you may be struggling is one of the biggest signs of strength.

Cherish every moment of your journey through fatherhood, even the less-than-desirable ones! Remember to capture as many experiences as you can, and make sure your partner is also in the photos. Time flies, and before you know it, your little one won't be so little anymore. Embrace every second, every giggle, and even every midnight wake-up call. These are the moments that mold your legacy.

TEST YOUR NEW DAD IQ: REFLECT ON FATHERHOOD

Once you get closer to your baby's first birthday, I want to encourage you to take some time to reflect on your journey through fatherhood this far. If it's still a few months to go, grab your phone and set a reminder to get back to this section. Reflection is extremely important to help you realize how far you've come since those octopus days when you felt too unco-ordinated to hold your baby. I'm convinced that you'll be absolutely amazed at the progress you've made, and realize that you truly deserve to wear your own super dad cape with pride.

I used to often postpone (or even put off) doing proper self-reflection, believing that there were more important things to do with my time. Then, I came across a quote by Canadian author Robin Sharma who famously wrote, "Awareness precedes choice and choice precedes change" (Sharma, n.d.). If we want to deliberately act in positive or helpful ways, we must make choices to support those actions. And, to make those choices, we need greater awareness of ourselves and our lives. I firmly believe practicing self-reflection and becoming more aware of both the positives and negatives in my life have helped me to become a better father, husband, and friend.

If you feel unsure of how to reflect on your amazing journey through the first year of fatherhood, take a moment to consider the man you were before your child's birth and the father you've become. Reflect on the shifts in your perspectives, priorities, and emotions. Use the prompts below to guide your introspection:

Before, now, and the future:

- Describe yourself in three words before your child was born.
- Now, choose three words that describe you as a father today.
- When you reflect on your journey in a year's time (when your child is two), which three words do you hope will describe you?
- What actions (if any) do you plan to take to get you closer to these three words?

Proudest moments:

- Jot down one specific instance where you felt immense pride in your role as a dad.
- What contributed to this proud moment?
- If you have anyone specific to thank for helping you create this moment, do so now. Even if this moment happened months ago and they might not remember

their input, you should still consider showing gratitude for the people on your journey.

Challenges overcame:

- Think of a difficult moment you've successfully navigated. What did it teach you?
- How did you overcome this challenge?
- If you were to face a similar struggle in the future, how would you tackle it?

Shift in priorities:

- List one thing that used to be crucial to you but has taken a backseat since becoming a father. How did this impact your life?
- What other things should you prioritize in the year ahead?

Emotional evolution:

- Describe an emotion or feeling you've only experienced since your child's birth.
- Have you become more comfortable with your emotions over this past year? If so, how?
- Are you still experiencing "New Dad Anxiety?" If not, how did you overcome it?

Fatherhood isn't a destination; it's a continuous voyage. You're equipped, you're prepared, and most importantly, you will rock as a dad! Keep growing, keep learning, and above all, keep loving. The adventure has only just begun.

If you enjoyed reading this book and found the information helpful in preparation for your journey, please leave us a 5-star review on Amazon, as your feedback can help another first-time father who is at the start of his journey, like you once were. Also, be sure to keep an eye out for my next and 3rd book, *You Will Rock as a Dad!: 85 New Dad Toddler Hacks* The Easy-To-Implement Young Dad Cheatsheet so that we can keep going on the journey of fatherhood together.

Thank you for coming on this journey with me once again.

Keep up that "rockin' dad energy"

Your friend,

~ Alex

REFERENCES

Ben-Joseph, E. P. (2018, June). *Breastfeeding vs. formula feeding (for parents)*. Kidshealth. https://kidshealth.org/en/parents/breast-bottle-feeding.html

Benefits of tummy time. (n.d.). Safe to Sleep. https://safetosleep.nichd.nih.gov/ reduce-risk/tummy-time

BetterHelp Editorial Team. (2024, January 25). *Understanding the facts about emotional memory*. BetterHelp. https://www.betterhelp.com/advice/ memory/understanding-the-facts-about-emotional-memory/

Bonding and attachment: Newborns. (2023, May 26). Raising Children Network. https://raisingchildren.net.au/newborns/connecting-communicat ing/bonding/bonding-newborns

Breastfeeding: How partners can help. (2022, October 11). Raising Children Network. https://raisingchildren.net.au/pregnancy/pregnancy-for-partners/ early-parenting/breastfeeding-partners-can-help

Brindle, D. (1999, June 16). Fathers under pressure to become superdads. *The Guardian*. https://www.theguardian.com/uk/1999/jun/16/davidbrindle

Canfield, K. (2007, April 27). *Dads of toddlers need patience*. National Center for Fathering. https://fathers.com/blog/your-kids/preschoolers/dads-of-toddlers-need-patience/

Canzater, S. L. (2019, July 11). *Talk to me, baby! The benefits of frequent, high-quality conversations with babies on brain and language development*. O'Neill Institute. https://oneill.law.georgetown.edu/talk-to-me-baby-the-benefits-of-frequent-high-quality-conversations-with-babies-on-brain-and-language-development/

CDC. (2021, February 22). *Toddlers (1-2 years old)*. Centers for Disease Control and Prevention. https://www.cdc.gov/ncbddd/childdevelopment/ positiveparenting/toddlers.html

FamilyEducation Editorial Staff. (2022, January 12). *Pressures of modern dads*. FamilyEducation. https://www.familyeducation.com/family-life/work/ unique-pressures-21st-century-dad

5 natural diaper rash remedies that actually work. (n.d.). Mustela. https://www. mustelausa.com/blogs/mustela-mag/natural-diaper-rash-remedies

Fontaine, D. (2023, December 22). *12 best natural remedies for eczema*. Medical News Today. https://www.medicalnewstoday.com/articles/324228

Gill, K. (2023, July 23). *How to get rid of cradle cap: Home remedies and when to seek help.* Healthline. https://www.healthline.com/health/parenting/how-to-get-rid-of-cradle-cap

HealthPartners. (2021, May 6). *13 tips for father-baby bonding.* HealthPartners. https://www.healthpartners.com/blog/tips-for-father-baby-bonding/

Horsager-Boehrer, R. (2021, August 17). *1 in 10 dads experience postpartum depression, anxiety: How to spot the signs.* UT Southwestern Medical Center. https://utswmed.org/medblog/paternal-postpartum-depression/

How many diapers do I need for a newborn? (2020, February 4). Munchkin. https://www.munchkin.com/blog/how-many-diapers-do-i-need-for-a-newborn/

Kreidman, J. (2023, January 20). *New dad anxiety - How to overcome the fear of fatherhood.* Dad University. https://www.daduniversity.com/blog/new-dad-anxiety-how-to-overcome-the-fear-of-fatherhood

Lee, J., Parikka, V., Lehtonen, L., & Soukka, H. (2021). Parent–infant skin-to-skin contact reduces the electrical activity of the diaphragm and stabilizes respiratory function in preterm infants. *Pediatric Research.* https://doi.org/10.1038/s41390-021-01607-2

Marcin, A. (2016, August 3). *How to hold a baby: Step by step.* Healthline. https://www.healthline.com/health/parenting/how-to-hold-a-newborn

Marple, K. (2022). *What's your new-father IQ?* BabyCenter. https://www.babycenter.com/family/fatherhood/new-father-iq_1325162

Mayo Clinic Staff. (2022, January 6). *Infant jaundice - Symptoms and causes.* Mayo Clinic. https://www.mayoclinic.org/diseases-conditions/infant-jaundice/symptoms-causes/syc-20373865

Mayo Clinic Staff. (2023, November 21). *Diaper rash - Symptoms and causes.* Mayo Clinic. https://www.mayoclinic.org/diseases-conditions/diaper-rash/symptoms-causes/syc-20371636

O'Connor, A. (2022, July 14). *Vitamins and breastfed babies.* What to Expect. https://www.whattoexpect.com/first-year/feeding-your-baby/vitamins-and-babies.aspx

Pacheco, D., & Wright, H. (2023, November 16). *Babies and sleep: What to expect & tips.* Sleep Foundation. https://www.sleepfoundation.org/baby-sleep

Patient. (n.d.). Merriam-Webster. https://www.merriam-webster.com/dictionary/patient#h1

Pitone, M. (2022, November). *Fevers.* Kids Health. https://kidshealth.org/en/parents/fever.html

Pitone, M. L. (2023, October). *Colic (for parents)*. Kids Health. https://kidshealth.org/en/parents/colic.html

Red flags by age for referral of a child. (2021). Help Me Grow. https://help megrowmn.org/HMG/GetHelpChild/WhenRefer/RedFlags/index.html

Sharma, R.S. (n.d.) *Robin S. Sharma quotes.* Good Reads. https://www.goodreads.com/quotes/289003-awareness-precedes-choice-and-choice-precedes-change

Skin-to-skin contact with newborns. (2021, April 6). Pampers. https://www.pampers.com/en-us/pregnancy/giving-birth/article/skin-to-skin-contact

Storring, C. (2021, October 1). *10 habits and practices to develop mindfulness for dads.* Dad.Work. https://dad.work/mindfulness-for-dads/

Tech Team. (2023, June 7). *Cloth diapers pros & cons: Cloth vs disposable diapers.* Nicki's Diapers. https://nickisdiapers.com/blogs/switch-to-sustain able/cloth-diapers-vs-disposable-cost-pros-cons

Tellado, M. P. (2023, September). *Oral thrush.* Kids Health. https://kidshealth.org/en/parents/thrush.html

The Bump Editors. (2018, May 2). *Diaper decisions: Cloth diapers vs. dispos-able.* The Bump. https://www.thebump.com/a/cloth-diapers-vs-disposable

The importance of celebrating tiny wins as a parent. (n.d.). Extraordinary Kids Pediatric Therapy Rhode Island. https://www.extraordinarykidstherapy.net/blog/the-importance-of-celebrating-tiny-wins-as-a-parent

Toffle, J. (2021, March 30). *Embracing imperfection as a parent and what I did about it.* Doctorpedia. https://www.doctorpedia.com/blog/embracing-imper fection-as-a-parent-and-what-i-did-about-it/

Villano, M. (2018, March 12). *When dad struggles after the baby arrives.* Seleni. https://www.seleni.org/advice-support/2018/3/12/when-dad-strug gles-after-the-baby-arrives

Made in United States
Troutdale, OR
10/14/2024

23769562R00080